Photoshop® Elements 2

Tom Arah
Barry Beckham
Adam Juniper
Todd Pierson
Paul Shipley

wrox

Photoshop® Elements 2
Published by
Wiley Publishing, Inc.
10475 Crosspoint Boulevard
Indianapolis, IN 46256
www.wiley.com

Copyright © 2003 by Wiley Publishing, Inc., Indianapolis, Indiana

Published simultaneously in Canada

Library of Congress Card Number: 2003107091

ISBN: 0-7645-4380-6

Manufactured in the United States of America

10 9 8 7 6 5 4 3 2 1

1R/RQ/QW/QT/IN

Credits

Content Architect
Adam Juniper

Project Manager
Jenni Harvey

Editor
Phill Jackson

Managing Editor
Sonia Mullineux

Graphic Editor
Ty Bhogal

Authors
Tom Arah
Barry Beckham
Adam Juniper
Todd Pierson
Paul Shipley

Indexer
Fiona Murray

Contents

 **Zero**   **1**

How to use this book 2
   Mac or PC? 3
   Styles 3
   Download 4
   Support 4
A bit of theory 5
   Color theory 5
   Alpha 6
   Printing 6
   ICC color profiles 6
Resolution 7
On with the show... 8
   Shortcut bar 9
   Toolbox 9
   Tool Options bar 10
   Palette Well 10
Palettes 11
   File Browser 11
   Hints & How To palettes 13
   Filters 14
   Effects 15
   Navigator palette 15
   Info palette 15
   Undo History palette 16
   Swatches 16
   Layers 17
   Layer Styles 17
Opening an image 17
   Zoom tool 18
   Changing the image size 20
Saving images 21
Phew! 22

⭐ **Overall image adjustments**   **23**

In this chapter 23
Rotating and cropping 24
   Rotating in the File Browser 24
   Rotating an opened image 25
   Rotating accurately with Layers 25
   Cropping using the Toolbox 27

Cropping accurately with the Options Bar 28
Cropping and rotating simultaneously 29
Cropping automatically 30
Brightness, contrast, and color 30
Brightness and contrast adjustment 31
Individual color adjustment with Levels 32
Color casts 36
Quick cast removal 37
Expert cast removal 37
Adding a cast with hue and saturation 38
Lighting 39
Lightening with Fill Flash 40
Backlighting adjustment 41
Recoloring 42
Focus sharpening 44

★2 Selection, copying and manipulation   **45**

In this chapter 45
Basic selection 46
Selecting an area 46
Deselecting an area 47
Selecting complicated shapes 48
Inverse selection 50
Complicated selection 50
Freehand shape selection 50
Angular shape selection 51
Automatic shape selection 52
Magic Wand 53
Anti-aliasing 55
Feathering 56
Selection Brush tool 57
Advertising ban 58
Moving and copying 59
Moving selections 59
Copying selections 60
Transforming selections 60
Perspective 63

Contents

⭐**3** ## Layers   **65**

In this chapter 65
Theory 66
Introduction to the Layers palette 67
   Customizing the palette 69
   Creating new layers 70
   Moving layers 70
   Duplicating layers 72
   Linking and merging layers 73
   Transparency 73
Adjustment layers 74
   Layer masks 76
   Masking shortcut keys 77
   Other adjustment layers 77
Layer management 78
   Naming layers 78
   Background layer 78
   Adjusting individual layers 79
   Flattening images 80
   Saving and exporting 81
Blending Modes 82
   Blending Mode effects 83
Layer Styles 89
   Preset styles 90
   Classic styles 91
   Removing styles 92
Cartoon time 92

⭐**4** ## Photo maniuplation   **97**

In this chapter 97
Clone Stamp tool 98
   Spot removal 98
   Delicate work 100
Dodging and burning 101
   Dodge tool 101
   Burn tool 102
Texture changes 102
   Blur tool 102
   Sharpen tool 103
   Sponge tool 103
   Smudge tool 103

Red Eye Brush tool 104
Doctoring images 105
    New skies 106
    Family photo 109
    Taking years off 114
Photomerge 120

5 Words and Pictures 127

In this chapter 127
How text is displayed 128
Adding text 129
    Using text from a word processor 131
    Shaping text 132
    Word and pictures 137
    Words from pictures 139
Shapes 141
    Using the shape tools 141
    Shape options 143
    Creating new shapes 143

6 Color, brushes, filters, and effects 147

In this chapter 147
The Brush tool 148
    Color pickers 148
    Different brushes 150
The Impressionist brush 152
Filters 154
    Using filters 154
    Useful filters 156
    Liquify filter 156
Effects 159
Aging an image 162
Spot color 164

Contents

7 **Outputting your work** **167**

In this chapter 167
Printing 168
   Simple printing 168
   Show More Options button 170
   Index print 170
   Picture packages 172
Exporting images 173
   Saving for the web 175
   Web gallery 177

Hero 1: Graphic Design Techniques **183**

Batch processing 183
   Basic image enhancement 188
   Filter-based styling 189
   Style-based formatting 195
   Layer-based copositing 197
   Brush-based painting 200
   Vector-based shape handling 203
   Applying the finishing touches 207
   Non-destructive color correction 208

Hero 2: Creative Art from Photographs **211**

In this chapter 211
Reducing resolution 213
Photo to watercolor 215
   Step 1: Cropping, cloning, and levels 216
   Step 2: Duplicate layer 217
   Step 3: Smart Blur and Soft Light 218
   Step 4: Filter 219
   Step 5: Re-adjusting tones 220
   Step 6: Selections 221
   Step 7: Copy and Paste patching 223
   Step 8: The Burn tool 225
Textures 226
Frames 227
   Step 1: Stroke command 228
   Step 2: Canvas size 229

Step 3: Color sampling and cloud effect 230
Step 4: Hue and saturation 230
Step 5: Adding Noise 231
Aging effect 231
Busker 234
Step 1: Plastic Wrap 234
Step 2: Cutout filter 235
Step 3: Merge layers 236
Step 4: Opacity 236
Step 5: Eraser 236
Step 6: Final tweaks 237

★ Hero 3: Fun Family Photographs　　239

In this chapter 239
The typical happy snap 240
Could we have done better? 240
Could we fix it in Elements? 240
Simplify your photos 241
Photo 3: Composition 242
Could we have done better? 243
Could we fix it in Elements? 243
Format 245
Could we have done better? 245
Could we fix it in Elements? 246
Distracting objects 246
Could we have done better? 246
Could we fix it in Elements? 246
Lighting 248
Motion 249
Could we have done better? 249
Could we fix it in Elements? 250
Tell a Story 251

★ Hero 4: Surreal Special Effects　　253

In this chapter 253
Finding a concept 255
The photography 255
Assembly of the elements 257
Details 263

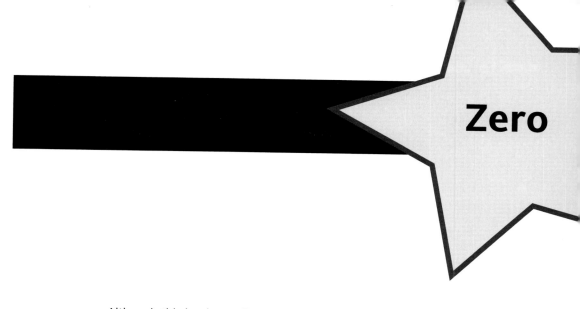

Zero

Although this book says *Zero* on the cover, we know that that's how your computer makes you feel, not what you are. And because of that feeling, this chapter is just for you. We'll look at all the stuff you really need to know about Photoshop Elements 2. Some of it isn't the easiest stuff in the world – there are one or two technical terms – but once you've got it out of the way, you can jump to any chapter in the book without any worries. After all, if you only want to clean up some red-eye in a photo, there's no point in this book forcing you to learn all about montage!

By the same token, as an author I don't propose to take this opportunity to tell you all about how many years I've been using Photoshop, how much I enjoy computers or which of my pet cats is my favorite. For a start, I don't have any cats, and secondly what's important is making *you* the hero here. (cape and tights sold separately).

How to use this book

As you've already gathered, this book is not an exercise in time wasting. Photoshop Elements 2 is a phenomenally capable application but it is also beautifully organized, which helps us out a lot. We've broken down the book into the best structure to get you going right away:

- ★ Chapter 'Zero'; this chapter, covers all the basic concepts you need to understand to get the best out of Photoshop. Once you've read this you'll have enough knowledge to tackle any other chapter in the book, in whatever order you choose.
- ★ Chapters one to seven; we've grouped all the things you actually want to do with Photoshop in appropriate chapters. They are arranged in order of ascending difficulty, but because the chapters are broken down into steps that you can follow and apply to your own images, you can dip in anywhere you like without finding yourself out of your depth.
- ★ Hero chapters; it's all very well being able to use the software, but sometimes you need that little extra. Rather than leave you high and dry, we've included four chapters by experienced professionals showing you how to put your skills together and create something really special.

And all the way through, you'll find every step clearly illustrated so you can see exactly what's going on.

Mac or PC?

Photoshop Elements 2 works on both Microsoft Windows (PCs) and Apple's Mac OS, and so does this book. As you can see, there is very little to distinguish the appearance of the two versions, except that the Windows version uses it's own self-contained window and the Mac version works directly above the desktop, just like pretty much every other program for the respective formats.

Although we'll use screenshots from both versions – as they're all interchangeable – we'll always put both keyboard shortcuts. For the most part, they're the same, but if you have to use a different key, we'll write the PC one then Mac one, either side of a '/', like this:

★ CTRL/⌘+C which is CTRL+C on a PC and ⌘+C on a Mac.
★ CTRL/⌘+SHIFT+C translates to CTRL+SHIFT+C on a PC and ⌘+SHIFT+C on a Mac.

The Photoshop file format can be read by both platforms.

▲Windows

▼Mac

Styles

In addition to using that special typeface for keyboard shortcuts, we'll use a few others as well, to make things a little clearer:

★ If we have any specific file types to mention, we'll write them like this.psd.
★ Menu commands are written out with little 'greater than' markers, e.g. Image > Resize > Canvas Size....
★ If we're mentioning an important technical term for the first time, we'll make it **obvious**.
★ And hyperlinks will appear like this www.friendsofed.com.

Really important points, and special tips, will appear in boxes like the one just to the right.

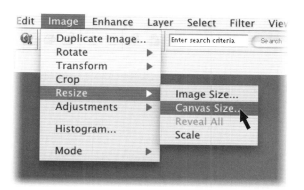

Yep, just here.

Download

This book is full of images and examples and, although it is designed for you to apply the techniques and effects to your own projects, you might want to follow along with ours. For that reason, we've made them available at www.friendsofed.com.

Support

All books from friends of ED should be easy to follow and error-free. However, if you do run into problems, don't hesitate to get in touch – our support is fast, friendly and free.

You can reach us at support@friendsofED.com, quoting the last for digits of the ISBN in the subject of the e-mail (that's 4232), and even if our dedicated support team are unable to solve your problem immediately, your queries will be passed on to the people who put the book together, the editors and authors, to solve. All our authors help with the support on their books, and will either directly mail people with answers, or (more usually) send their response to an editor to pass on.

We'd love to hear from you, even if it's just to request future books, ask about friends of ED, or tell us how much you loved *Photoshop Elements 2 Zero to Hero!*

If your enquiry concerns an issue not directly concerned with book content, then the best place for these types of questions is our message board list at http://www.friendsofed.com/forums. Here, you'll find a variety of people talking about what they do and who should be able to provide some ideas and solutions.

For news, more books, sample chapters, downloads, author interviews and more, send your browser to www.friendsofED.com.

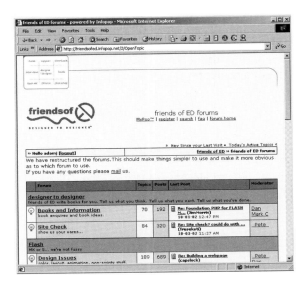

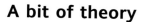

A bit of theory

Sorry about this, folks, but there are a couple of concepts we really need to nail down before we get our hands dirty. If they haven't come up already, they will at some point, and there is a lot of misinformation floating around about them both.

Color theory

This is a topic on which the experienced professional could be drawn for hours. Complete books have been written about it. But don't worry, we won't be getting into anything like that deep!

You probably already know that your computer monitor, like your television, mixes Red Green and Blue to produce every other color you see on the screen. This process is called **additive color**, as all three colors mix to create perfect white.

This does not, in fact, produce the infinite range of color that we can see with the human eye, because we don't see things in quite the same way. In the real world, a full spectrum of color radiates from a light source – usually the sun – and we see what is reflected from an object.

If we lose some of that whole spectrum, we lose a few colors here and there, for example the 'fluorescent marker' style colors aren't well represented. The shades that can be represented are known as a **color space**.

Within the color space, the number of different shades available to you is determined by the number of **bits per pixel**. A 'bit' is the smallest unit of a computer's memory, and so the more bits you allow for each unit of the image (pixel), the more possible shades of that color.

In Photoshop, except for certain specific things, images are represented in 24-bits per pixel, or **24-bit color**. That is 8 bits (256 possible shades) for each color, a maximum of 16.8 million colors.

> *Whenever you see this* ✪ *star symbol, the image can also be found in the color section.*

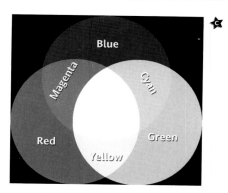

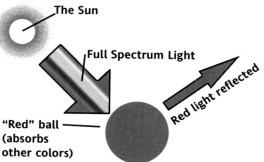

The Sun

Full Spectrum Light

Red light reflected

"Red" ball (absorbs other colors)

Alpha

Of course, there is no need to stop at 24-bit color, and in some cases you may see devices advertised with even higher levels. Be warned though; these things are not always what they seem.

32-bit color doesn't mean 10 and two-thirds bits per pixel, instead it retains the 24-bits for the three color shades and also defines a level of transparency, again from 256 possible shades. This is known as an **alpha channel**, and we'll see how useful it can be later.

Printing

If everything about color space seemed a little involved, don't worry, it doesn't come up a lot in Photoshop Elements. It's important, though, as there are different ways of making up color, and the most obvious one you'll encounter is your printer.

Your printer uses **subtractive color**, in that it works away from white (the opposite of RGB) and it uses variants of the primary colors that you remember from nursery school, Magenta, Cyan and Yellow, or **CMYK**. The 'K' on the end stands for Key, and means black. Theoretically, the primary colors should mix to form a perfect black, but in reality you often get muddy browns, so most manufacturers (and professional printers) use a separate ink.

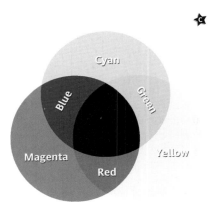

These days, some printers use more colors to make mixing easier, but, luckily, you don't really have to worry about this as the printer driver software should deal with these things for you.

ICC color profiles

Because every device that deals with color, from scanners and digital cameras, through monitors and eventually to the printer can get things a little wrong when measuring color, an impartial scientific standard was created, called the ICC (International Color Consortium) profile.

Basically, the software supplied with any device also stores it's ICC profile, to enable your computer can make allowances at every stage so that, in theory, the colors you see on the screen are those that appear on the page.

You can turn this facility on in Photoshop by clicking Edit > Color Settings... (CTRL/⌘+SHIFT+K) and selecting 'Full color management', but, unless you're confident that all your devices have such profiles, we'd advise against it. Your printer will undoubtedly come with software that makes optimized translation between screen and print colors so, to be honest, it usually works out best not to over-complicate things.

Resolution

Many people get a long way through their understanding of Photoshop without ever fully getting to grips with resolution, but it is well worth doing.

In it's simplest terms, the resolution of an image is its level of detail – the higher the resolution the better quality the image, but the larger the file size.

Resolution is measured in dots per inch (or pixels per inch), which tell the computer how large to draw the image on the printed page. (Or, how large the area each pixel – individual color square – represents.) As a rule of thumb, 300dpi is about as good as you'll need to get.

Where things get complicated is when you want to change the resolution of an image. Though Photoshop is capable of scaling the resolution, any change – especially an increase – has a slight blurring effect. The example was reduced from the 300dpi image on the right to the 72dpi one on the left.

These images show what happens when you try to scale up the image using either the 'Bicubic', or the 'Neatest Neighbor', method. Bicubic does the blurring effect to simulate a higher resolution, but the Nearest Neighbor method just zooms the pixels into a mosaic pattern. Both methods are available from the Image > Resize > Image Size...

72dpi   **300dpi**

Original

Zoomed (Neighbor)   Zoomed (Bicubic)

menu (discussed in a moment) but let's meet the program now.

On with the show...

Without further ado, let's get going. If you've not installed your copy of Photoshop yet, now's the time; just put the CD Rom into the drive and follow the on-screen instructions. There's no reason not to use the standard, or 'easy' install option, everything is definitely included that way.

Open up your copy now, and we'll get acquainted with the user interface. As we've said, it might not look quite the same, depending on your version of your operating system, but the main elements are all there:

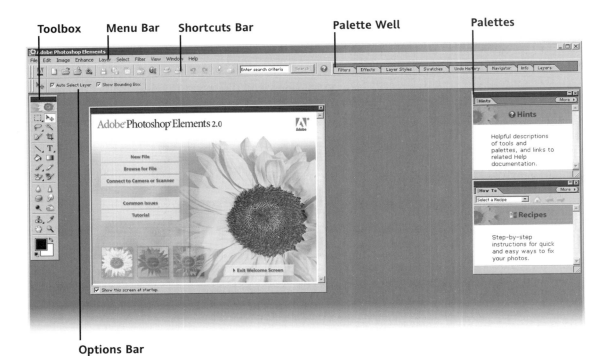

Toolbox **Menu Bar** **Shortcuts Bar** **Palette Well** **Palettes**

Options Bar

Now, you'll be familiar with the concept of the menu bar from your other software. As for the rest, we'll have a look at these point by point.

Shortcut bar

This tucks away all those essentials — Save, Load, Print etc. — and remains ever present. Just click on one of the buttons, as you would with the toolbar in a word processor.

Toolbox

Most of the buttons that actually do something are stored in the Toolbox, which originally appears on the left of the screen.

It contains all the tools you will need to select areas of your image, edit them, change your view of it and "paint" on it. Some of the tools actually have a number of others hidden underneath them. These tools are indicated with a small black triangle at the bottom-right of their icon. If you click and hold on one of these buttons, a menu will appear allowing you to select any of the other tools that were tucked away. Once you've selected one of these concealed tools, it remains the 'top' tool from its submenu.

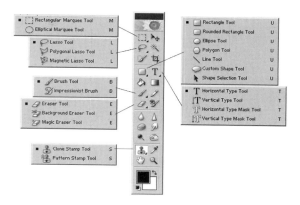

You can also select Toolbox tools using keyboard shortcuts, like E for Eraser, and pressing the SHIFT key at the same time allows you to select one of the hidden tools.

At the top of the toolbox is a sunflower button that links directly to the Adobe website, which you can click on to get updates etc.

At the bottom, is the color picker, which shows the currently selected Foreground and Background colors (black and white by default). The foreground color applied to shapes, brushes and text you add, the Background is used by the Eraser tool if you are working on the background layer.

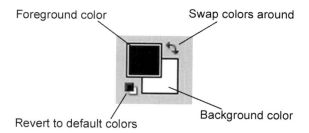

Foreground color — Swap colors around — Revert to default colors — Background color

If you click on the arrow button in the top right-hand corner of the square, the colors are swapped. The button in the opposite corner resets the colors to their defaults.

Clicking on either colored square brings up the Photoshop color picker. You can select a color by dragging the slider (near the middle) to any hue that you want. Once you're happy with that color, then click anywhere inside the shaded square to select your choice of color. As you can see, the colors tend towards each other in the corners.

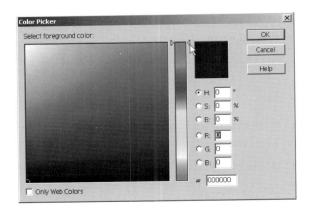

If you click the 'Only Web Colors' check box in the bottom-left, then the window will only display one of the 216 colors that can safely be displayed on all web browsers; handy if you're preparing graphics for the internet.

You can also enter values into either the HSB, RGB or Hexadecimal (#) boxes on the right. The latter is especially handy if you've been working on web graphics in another program, as hexadecimal is the standard way of describing web colors.

Alternatively, you can select the Eyedropper tool from the Toolbox, and click in your image on a pixel that is the color you wish to select.

Tool Options bar

This bar sits beneath the Shortcuts bar at the top of the screen, and changes to reflect the tool currently selected in the Toolbox. That tool's icon is repeated on the far left of the Tool Options bar, followed by appropriate option buttons.

Palette Well

To the right of the Shortcuts bar is the Palette Well. This is where Photoshop stores palettes (small windows of tools, which we'll see in a minute) when they're not in use, much like putting your toys back in your cupboard.

Each tab represents a palette, which can be clicked and dragged out into your desktop to be viewed full size, or just clicked on to be used briefly. On smaller monitors, Photoshop doesn't have room to display all the palettes in the Well, so the rest are accessible via the Window > menu.

Palettes

The palettes are a core part of Photoshop's functionality. Each acts like a little window, mimicking those around them in either Mac OS or Windows. They contain easy access to a special set of tools that you can use to achieve certain effects. We'll have a quick look at each, so you can familiarize yourself with the possibilities of the software. You can always reset the palettes to their original locations by clicking Window > Reset Palette Locations.

File Browser

We'll start with an exception to the rule. The File Browser palette is accessed from it's own button (highlighted in the picture) towards the left-hand end of the Shortcuts bar.

The File Browser is made up of a number of panes. In the top left is a directory tree, of a sort your probably familiar with from other applications on your computer.

The main window, on the right, holds previews of all the images that Photoshop understands in the folder you have selected using the directory tree. A single-click on any of these makes it the selected image, and its details are then transferred to the panes on the bottom-left of the window. A double-click opens the image for editing in Photoshop.

In common with other palettes, the File Browser can be resized just like any other window. All palettes also have an array of options along the bottom, and a More button in the top right.

By clicking on the More button, we bring up a menu option allowing us to, for example, reduce the size of the thumbnails. We could also create a New Folder, rotate our selected image (though the effects only take place when the image is opened fully by Photoshop and changes are saved) or even open the window in our native operating system.

Some of these options can be accessed by clicking on the buttons along the bottom of the palette too. For example, clicking once on an image's thumbnail selects it, then clicking once on the trash-can icon in the bottom right deletes that image. You can make other permanent changes to the contents of your disc, for example by dragging a thumbnail into a different folder in the directory tree. That has the effect of moving the image into that folder.

But that's not all – by clicking and dragging our pointer along the dividing lines between panes within the File Browser, we can resize them to suit our purposes.

When you close the File Browser, using the close 'x' in Windows (red button in Mac OS X) it will retain your settings, and can be brought back at any time by clicking on the File Browser button in the Shortcuts bar as before.

Hints & How To palettes

Both of these palettes are opened by default in Photoshop, but we won't be making much use of them in this book. They are, you see, designed to assist people without the presence of mind to buy a book on the subject. But, as we hope you'll soon agree, they are a bit of a poor second.

The **Hints** palette works by keeping an eye on what tool you have selected in the Toolbox, and indeed sometimes on the options you have selected in the Options bar too. It then provides a brief description of the purpose of the tool you have selected and, under the heading-related topics, a number of hyperlinks to pages in Photoshop's internal help.

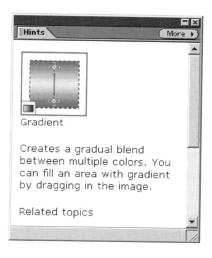

This is all very useful. However, by clicking on one of these links not only do you have to wait for Explorer to load, but if you wish to read the instructions, you will probably find that it takes up the majority of the space on your computer monitor.

What we can do, however, is stop these two palettes cluttering up our valuable screen space by tucking them behind one another.

Simply click on the **How To** tab at the top left of the palette (or vice versa), and drag it somewhere inside the Hints palette, as pictured. The two palettes will then join together in the same window, with the tabs nestling behind each other, much as in the Palette Well.

While we've got it open, let's have a nose at the **How To** palette as well. It is designed to alleviate the screen space problem with the online help providing you with "recipes" (brief step-by-step instructions) inside the palette window. In fact the palette itself acts like a mini web-browser, with forward, back and home buttons at the top.

The palette can also be asked to do some of the steps of some recipes for you, taking the chores out of some tasks. Naturally this is at the expense of your own involvement so, while they seem like a great idea at first, you'll soon find them stifling your creativity.

To some extent, this problem can be alleviated. At the top of the palette there is a drop-down menu which contains a number of groupings of recipes. The bottom-most option is one to download new recipes from the Adobe web site. Clicking on it jumps to a wizard which is remarkably fast, even on a slow connection.

At the end of the day, though, neither of these palettes are present in Photoshop 7 (Element's elder brother), they have both been tacked on to help users get to grips with the software, not unlike calling you a Dummy! If you use this book, you shouldn't find yourself needing to resort to either of them, plus you'll probably need that space for some of the more useful palettes.

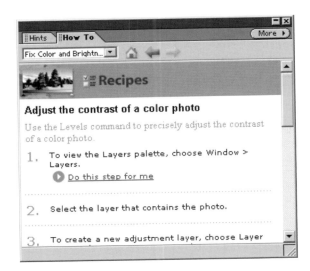

Filters

The Filters palette is a great way of changing a whole image really quickly. A 'filter' is geek-speak for applying a mathematical formula to all the pixels that make up an image, and over the years more and more complicated formulae have been devised with more and more impressive effects.

As with the recipes, they are grouped by means of the drop-down menu on the top-left (though you can select 'All' and view every one at once). Some blur an image, others create lighting effects.

At the top the 'Filter Options' when checked ensures that, if there are adjustable settings for the filter you have selected, then you are shown them. If unchecked, Photoshop just uses the defaults. At the bottom the two buttons on the bottom-right allow you to change your view of the palette.

Effects

Much the same as filters, though for the most part more decorative. The Effects palette is used in exactly the same way – select from the available categories then double-click (or press 'Apply') to use the Effect you have chosen.

Many of the effects here take a few moments to compute as they are made up of other effects, or could be achieved using other methods in the program. That said, on occasions the boarders or even the Ink Blots can be quite effective. Just don't get carried away – some members of your family might not appreciate Green Slime added to their favorite pictures, however well you feel it represents your sister.

Navigator palette

The Navigator palette is designed to give you a small thumbnail of the picture you're currently working on. The red border (though you can change it's color from the More menu) shows the edge of the area currently visible – in this case the whole image. By typing a figure into the bottom-left box, or adjusting the slider between the mountain icons, we can adjust the zoom level, much like using a camera with a zoom lens.

When we are not viewing the whole image in our main window, we can drag the rectangle around the thumbnail in the Navigator palette in order to adjust out view accordingly.

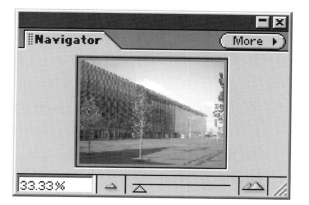

Info palette

This palette keeps its eye on the position of the mouse pointer, reporting back the details of the color underneath the pointer (in RGB decimal and hexadecimal), and the position of the pointer in the preferred distance measurement.

The More menu includes a Palette Options... dialog which allows the user to adjust this information to suit.

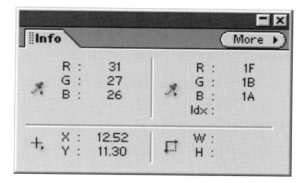

Undo History palette

Computer users have grown used to being able to easily undo mistakes with their software, and Photoshop is no exception. In addition to the traditional Ctrl/⌘+Z for undo (though the actual buttons are adjustable in the Preferences dialog), Photoshop also includes an Undo History palette.

This palette stores the most recently used tools (20 steps, by default) and allows you to step back and forward through them. For example, in this screenshot here, we have undone our use of the Eraser to go back to just after using the Crop tool. Until we make another change, we can redo by clicking on the Eraser entry again.

If 20 steps seems somewhat limiting, and you have spare memory or hard disc pace, you can increase your number of undos by clicking Ctrl/⌘+K and altering the figure in the 'History States' box.

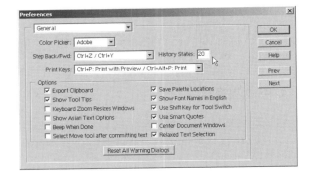

Swatches

Earlier we touched upon the topic of color, and specifically that we could change the foreground and background colors by clicking on them in the Toolbox.

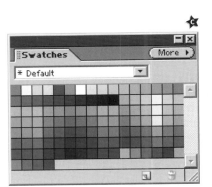

The Swatches palette is for those of us who find ourselves using color a lot. You can select from a number of color swatches using the drop-down menu at the top, or add the current foreground color to your swatch by clicking on the New Swatch button on the bottom. (If you press Shift at the same time, the background color will be added.)

You can also delete colors by means of the 'trash can' at the bottom, but unless you save from the More> menu, you will not make any permanent alterations.

Layers

Without doubt, one of the most important features of Photoshop is layers. It enables you to build up an image in much the same way an animator might use sheets of acetate. A good example is the shot of the Shortcut bar that accompanied the File Browser above. There a final image was built up out of two layers, one viewed at half opacity, with a transparent 'hole' cut in it to create a spotlight effect.

But you need not stop at two layers, Photoshop allows the use of hundreds of layers, and it allows you to apply different effects to different layers. Here we can be seen adjusting the opacity of 'Layer 1'. We could also have given the layer shadow effects, a glowing halo, or even adjusted the way that it interacted with layers below it. Suffice to say, there will be a bit more on layers in the rest of the book.

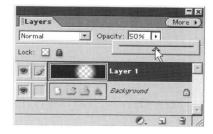

Layer Styles

Hand in hand with Layers are Layer Styles (in fact, many users choose to nestle this palette behind their Layers one, as we did with How to and Hints). This palette works much like the Filters or Effects ones, except that the styles are applied to individual layers and they leave the content of the layer editable.

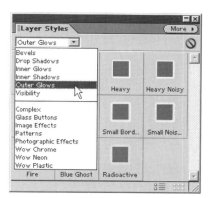

For example, If you had a layer with some words in it, and you'd used Layer Styles to apply a drop shadow, then you could still edit the text and the Layer Style would adjust itself to follow suit.

You can apply one of each of the top six categories in the drop-down menu, and/or use one of the pre-defined ones in the bottom half.

Opening an image

Right, we've seen what we can do, but we've barely even opened a picture yet. Photoshop is capable of opening a bewildering variety of different image types, but the main ones for our purposes are:

★ **JPEG** is pretty much the standard image type from modern digital cameras, and common for photographic images on the Internet. JPEG is a 'lossy' compression format, which means it loses some detail in order to save space when saving. The level of compression can be selected by the user.

★ **TIFF** is a high-end standard, used where absolute quality is important, but, because it is uncompressed, it takes up a lot of file space.

★ **PSD** is the Photoshop and Photoshop Elements standard file type. This is the only format that will correctly store layers, editable text etc.

Photoshop will open pretty much every other standard file type, including GIF, BMP, EPS, PCX, PDF, Photo CD, PICT, PXR, PNG, TGA and WBMP.

Zoom tool

1. To open an image, locate an image using the File Browser and double-click on it.

2. Now locate and select the Zoom tool (magnifying glass) at the bottom-right of the Toolbox.

Notice how the Options bar changes to reflect the tool you have selected.

Alternatively, you can get an image directly from any digital devices you may have attached to your computer (Scanner, Digital Camera etc.) by clicking File > Import > *and selecting the names of any devices you have installed.*

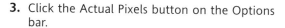

3. Click the Actual Pixels button on the Options bar.

The view scale in the title bar of the image should change to (or remain at) 100%. You can also find this information in the Navigator palette, and at the far-left of the info bar (at the bottom of the Elements window in Windows, at the bottom of the Live Image window in Mac OS).

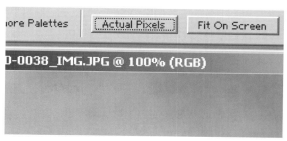

4. Click the Print Pixels button on the Options Bar.

The image on screen scale will change to roughly reflect the size it would print at. If it stays at 100%, then it must be exactly the same resolution as your monitor (either 72 or 96dpi).

5. Now, with the Zoom tool still selected, click somewhere in your image, drag the mouse to another point to form a rectangle, then let go.

Photoshop will zoom into your picture at the closest scale that fits the whole of the rectangle you drew onto the screen. Zooming the image, using any of the methods shown above, will not affect the size or appearance of the image on the disc.

> *Because of simple mathematics, a pictures will look better when zoomed to 25%, 50%, 100% or 200% etc. as these are divisions or multiplications of scale by a whole, even number. Viewing at 66%, for example, might look a little jaggier on screen, but doesn't affect the final quality either.*

Changing the image size

Resolution was discussed at the beginning of the chapter. Pressing Image > Resize > Image Size... lets you make changes to it:

This brings up a dialog box which allows you to make a number of adjustments to the image:

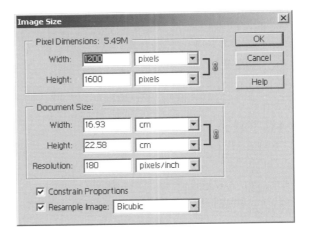

* ★ You can adjust the Pixel Dimensions by typing in a new Width or Height. This changes the level of detail of the image.
* ★ You can use the drop-down menus to the right of the dimensions boxes (marked 'pixels' in the screenshot) to adjust the scale of the dimensions.
* ★ If you make changes to the dimensions in the Document Size pane, then the pixels will be changed to reflect your changes. You can also alter the final resolution here, and the final effect on the size of the image will be calculated for you.
* ★ The Constrain Proportions box toggles whether the two dimensions will be adjusted in proportion to each other (represented also by the chain link drawn to the right of each pair of figures).
* ★ The Resample Image check means that the pixels of the image will be altered when OK is clicked, according to the method selected in the drop-down menu, e.g. Bicubic, which produces smoothed edges. With Resample Image turned off, only the resolution of the image will be changed. Resolution is only an instruction to the computer telling it what size each pixel should be at final output.

Saving images

The only thing we've not properly covered that you'll need to know is how to save files. Photoshop is capable of saving in a large number of different file formats, though the most important is its own – the PSD – which it shares with it's bigger brother, Photoshop 7.

To save a file, click File > Save..., or CTRL/⌘+S. To save a file under a different format from the one you opened it in, click File > Save As..., or CTRL/⌘+SHIFT+S.

Here you can choose an appropriate format. It is worth bearing in mind that only the PSD format retains the image fully editable, with layers and text still editable. Almost all the other file formats have certain other advantages, but if you ever expect to come back to your work, have a PSD copy as well.

JPEG is the format preferred by most modern digital cameras, as it is designed to store images in as small an amount of disc or memory space as possible. The result of this is a certain amount of jaggedness, or "artifacts", around edges in an image. When you save a JPEG in Photoshop, you are offered certain quality settings – the lowest produces the lowest file size, but also the most obvious artifacts.

In our examples, the qualities (out of 12) are shown at the bottom. The file sizes are 32k, 25k and 23k respectively, though sometimes the difference can be more marked than that.

9/12   5/12   1/12

The salient point is this, JPEG is a great way to save files to e-mail to your friends and family (more details in Chapter 7), but PSD is the way to store your work without any loss of quality. If you have a CD-Writer, CDs are a very inexpensive way of backing up your work from time to time (and more waterproof than old fashioned prints, as I learned to my cost a few years ago).

Phew!

Wow, there was a lot in that last few pages. Don't worry, we're not expecting you to remember any of the detail of it. It just seemed like a good idea to show you around, and get a few of the concepts of working with pictures in computers floating around in your mind. Now your route forward is up to you; feel free to flick through the pages looking for a project that appeals to you, or if you have time to digest a more comprehensive understanding then follow each chapter in order. Above all, remember to enjoy it!

Overall image adjustments

One

In this chapter

In this chapter, we'll be taking a look at the things that you can do to change the overall impression that your image gives. These are the topics we'll be covering:

★ Rotation
★ Cropping
★ Brightness
★ Contrast
★ Color levels
★ Color casts
★ Hue/Saturation
★ Lightening
★ Backlighting
★ Recoloring
★ Sharpening

Rotating and cropping

Rotating images is often an act of necessity, as digital cameras and scanners often save them the wrong way up. Cropping, on the other hand is more of a luxury – no less easy, but used to emphasize a subject or, in extreme cases, remove one.

Rotating in the File Browser

An easy way to rotate an image that has been scanned sideways or upside down is to use the Rotate button in the File Browser:

1. Select the File Browser from the Shortcuts bar. (The icon of a folder and magnifying glass 🔍)

2. Use the directory tree to open the folder that contains the image you wish to rotate.

3. Click once on the image that you want to rotate.

4. To rotate it once to the right, click on the Rotate button at the bottom right of the window (as pictured). This will only affect the image when opened in Photoshop – a point that the software will make to you by way of a warning message.

   You can also rotate the image to the left by holding down the ALT key as you press the Rotate button.

5. The image will then be rotated in the File Browser.

6. Double-click on the image to open it. This is when the whole image (as opposed to just the thumbnail) will be rotated.

7. To keep the changes, be sure to save the image when prompted by Photoshop.

This is a handy technique because it works on the thumbnails, but it only works in 90° steps, and you still have to open and close the images to save the changes.

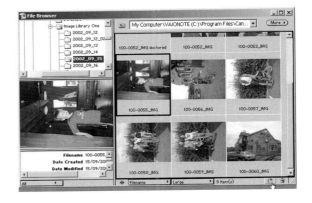

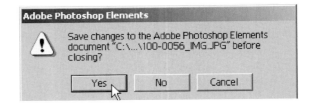

Rotating an opened image

You aren't forced to use the File Browser to quickly rotate an image. You can also use the menu options under the Image menu. We won't insult your intelligence by explaining what 90° Left, 90° Right and 180° mean. Custom... merely allows you to enter your own value anywhere in between. When you use this function, Photoshop fills around your new angled image with the currently selected background color (at the bottom of your Toolbox), so you may find the technique below slightly more manageable!

The Flip tools, on the other hand flip the image like a mirror. Sometimes this is useful for printing onto T-Shirts, but its best to follow the instructions provided with your T-Shirt transfer paper.

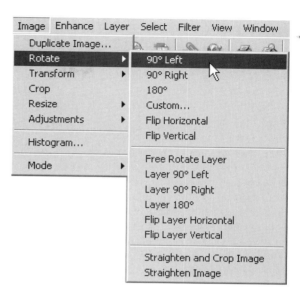

Rotating accurately with Layers

More advanced rotation is slightly hampered by the way computers think: in square pixels. It's simple to just move an image around by 90° because its basic building blocks have 90° edges too.

This picture of an office block has been taken by a careless photographer and appears to lean over slightly to the right. We can use Photoshop, with a careful eye, to correct this.

1. Open the image you wish to rotate into Photoshop, either from the File Browser, or using the File > Open... menu.

2. Select Image > Rotate > Free Rotate Layer. If you are working on an image you've just opened, it might not have layers (a necessity for rotation). In that case, Photoshop will ask you to make the image a layer – use whatever name it suggests.

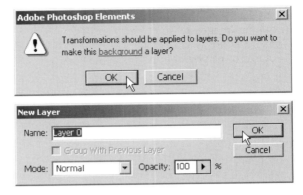

3. You should now find that your layer is surrounded by thin, solid lines and when you move the pointer near to a corner, a two-ended arrow appears. (If not, try repeating the first part of *step 2*).

4. When a pointer like this (bottom left) appears, click and drag and the whole image will be rotated. Alternatively, you can enter values into the Options bar at the top of the screen if you prefer or need the extra accuracy.

5. Once you are happy with the state of your image, click on the tick at the end of the Options Bar. Photoshop will then smooth out the rough 'draft' it did while you were still adjusting the angle.

6. The final image *may* have a gray-checkered pattern around it – this is how Photoshop represents transparency. We can sort this out by cropping the image with the Crop tool...

Cropping using the Toolbox

Cropping images in Photoshop is extremely easy. The Crop tool is located towards the top of the Toolbox, or can be accessed by simply pressing the C key (except when using the Text tool).

1. Open the image you wish to crop.

2. Select the Crop tool from the Toolbox.

3. Move the mouse pointer to a corner of the rectangular area of the image you wish to retain.

4. Click and drag, releasing the mouse when you reach the opposite diagonal corner of the area you want to keep.

5. The area surrounding your picture will then be grayed over, but it's all still there. You can still adjust the area to be cropped by clicking in one of the squares around the rectangle.

6. When you are happy, click on the tick at the right hand end of the Options Bar. This performs the crop.

You will be left with your cropped image. Bear in mind that your cropped image won't have as much detail as the original, if scaled up to the same size.

Cropping accurately with the Options Bar

An alternative to using the click and drag method described above is to type the size of your desired final image into the Options Bar. This is really useful when you know exactly what size paper you need to print onto, or what size image you need for a web page.

1. Open the image you wish to crop, as before, and select the Crop tool.

2. Type the dimensions of your final intended image, adding the measurements you are using. Common ones are:

   - ★ in for inches
   - ★ cm for centimeters
   - ★ px for pixels

3. Remember to type the resolution that you want your final image to be. In this example, we'll use 300ppi for a photo quality print.

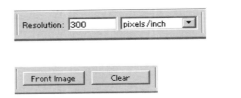

   (You can clear any dimensions or resolution you have added by pressing the Clear button to the right of the Options Bar. The Crop tool will then resume acting as in the above example.)

4. Now click and drag over the area that you want to print. This time, the proportions of height and width are fixed, and the other corner won't exactly follow the pointer.

5. As before, click the tick at the end of the Options Bar when you're ready and the area you've chosen will be made into an image of the dimensions and resolution you chose. Photoshop will handle any scaling automatically.

Cropping and rotating simultaneously

As shown previously, in the *Rotating accurately with Layers* section, one of the problems with rotating an image is that you can be left with an odd shaped image. The solution to this is to crop and rotate at the same time.

1. Open the image you wish to crop, then, as in the previous example, select the Crop tool.

2. Use one of the methods described above to highlight the rough region you want to crop, but don't press the tick yet.

3. Now, as you move the pointer near the edges of your image, you'll notice that it turns into a two-way arrowhead. When it is in this state, click and drag to rotate your rectangle.

4. Afterwards, you can still adjust the corner points by clicking and dragging from inside them.

5. When you're happy with the area you are going to select, click the tick button on the Options Bar to perform the operation.

It's worth noting that all of these rotation routines can sometimes slightly degrade image quality, as one grid pattern of pixels (the original image) is being asked to fit onto another (the new angle). Although Photoshop will try its best to compensate, the result won't retain exactly the same level of detail as the original.

Cropping automatically

If you don't fancy all the mouse clicks involved in cropping and rotating (we reckon it can be as many as four) you can ask Photoshop to do it for you. Not that it'll make a very good job of it, mind you.

Click Image > Rotate > Straighten and Crop Image and Photoshop will take a look at the image, and often just give up! Other times it gets confused and makes a slightly wonky image far worse.

Where it does work is with images with a clearly defined foreground and clean lines. Photoshop will, on those rare occasions, make a reasonable stab at identifying what isn't needed (for example sky) and cropping it. Don't say you've not been warned.

Brightness, contrast, and color

One of the most effective, and easiest, changes you can make to an image is to alter its colors or shades. There are any number of reasons you might want to do this, all equally valid. Here are a few:

- ★ The image seems too dark, or too light. Perhaps it has been badly exposed.
- ★ An area of the image has been flooded with the flash.
- ★ The image has a colorcast (i.e. it tends towards a specific color).
- ★ The image has scanned badly, and the colors don't seem like the original.

Not only will Photoshop make these tasks quick and simple, but it will also allow you varying degrees of control depending on how much you want to get your hands dirty. The classic example is between the Brightness/Contrast and Levels, so let's take a look at both; easiest first.

Brightness and contrast adjustment

This picture of Birmingham University is hideously underexposed, thanks to careless use of the camera's "manual" mode. It can be corrected a number of ways, but first we'll try the Brightness/Contrast slider.

1. Open your faulty image (or use ours from the download).

2. Open the Brightness/Contrast dialog from the Enhance > Adjust Brightness/Contrast > Brightness/Contrast… menu.

3. Adjust the sliders by clicking and dragging on them. Given the state of this image, they both need to be moved a long way!

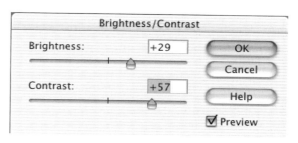

4. When happy, click OK and the change will be made.

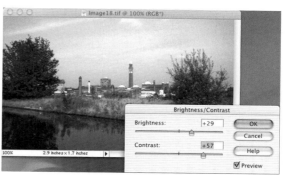

You can make some quick and effective changes to the image in this way, and if the Preview box is checked, then the change will appear instantaneously. The problem is that it isn't very exacting. While you might use the brightness and contrast buttons to adjust your TV, the studios have many more complicated ways of perfecting the picture. Photoshop lets us get a bit nearer to the action in that respect, and a much better way of adjusting the contrast is to use the Levels dialog.

Individual color adjustment with Levels

Levels works by showing you a histogram of the various amounts of different shades in the image (ignoring the hues, for the time being). Along the bottom – the X axis, for the mathematically inclined – all the possible shades, from black to white are drawn. The height – up the Y axis – represents the amount of that sort of shade. For example, the image on the right is a histogram of a picture that doesn't have many very dark pixels (hence the lowness of the chart on the left), has a lot of mid-range colors and quite a few very bright pixels – note the peak at the far right, bright white.

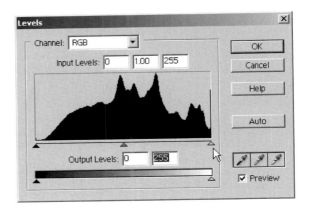

Why is this useful? Well, the three triangles at the bottom of the histogram, representing lowlights, midtones and highlights, can be adjusted. If, for example, we move the lowlights (leftmost) triangle a little to the right, then Photoshop would take this new point as the darkest point in the image, and adjust the other pixels accordingly.

Oh, and one other point – there is no ideal to aim for here. The histogram shows you where there are, and are not, shades in your image – and depends greatly on the subject, weather etc. For example, a picture taken at night is likely to have more dark shades, so look a little left-heavy on the histogram.

Confused? Thought so, we'd better try it out so you can see what's going on:

1. Open an image, preferably one without much contrast, or that is too dark/light. This picture has too many dark shades, and too many bleached ones (as we can see from the histogram).

2. Open the Levels panel by clicking CTRL/⌘+L, or click Enhance > Adjust Brightness/Contrast > Levels....

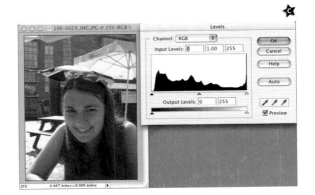

3. Now bring the lowlights slider in slightly to the right, so that it is underneath the first big peak in the histogram. Do this by clicking and dragging on it.

4. As the girl's face is in a darker area of the image, and nothing very important is in a lighter area, we can afford to bring the Highlights slider much further.

5. That's better, but the face is still a little muddy in the midtones, and we need to lighten that a little. Drag the midtones slider to the left (so that more of the midtones end up lying between the midtones and highlights sliders).

If you go wrong at any point, you don't need to click Cancel and start again. As in many other dialogs in Photoshop, simply hold down the ALT key, and the Cancel button will temporarily become a Reset button, that sets the sliders back to their starting point.

6. When you're happy with the results, click OK.

Just for fun, open the Levels dialog again. You'll notice that the new histogram looks a little like a bar code. The reason is that when Photoshop "stretched" the color tones we had selected between our new light and dark points (which now have huge peaks), it did it all mathematically and so, in places, just left gaps.

When we made our changes, all the points below the lowtones slider became black and all the points above the highlights slider became white (hence two very tall narrow peaks at either end of the new histogram. By adjusting the midtones slider, we lightened the shades of the image by moving more colors into the top half of the slider (hence the darker, more solid part of the histogram there).

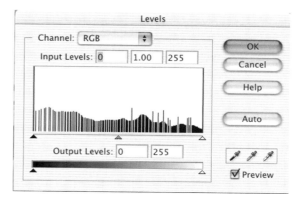

While this isn't a problem straight away, as we're left with an image that looks a lot better, it can start to show up if we make repeated use of the Levels dialog. The trick is to keep an original, and go back to that if you're not happy (or use Adjustment Layers, which are covered in Chapter 3).

Also, at this point it is worth mentioning the Output Levels slider at the bottom. This allows you to prevent the final bar chart from stretching right to the darkest, or lightest, possible shades of color. Drag the arrows beneath in a little to set a light/dark limit. You can even cross them over to get a negative effect, if you like.

Quick Levels

There are a couple of ways to speed things up while you're using the Levels commands. One is those little eyedroppers towards the bottom right of the dialog, which can be a little hit and miss.

1. Open an image in need of adjustment (we'll use the university example from earlier) and open the Levels dialog (CTRL/⌘+L).

2. Click on the Set Black Point (leftmost) eyedropper, and then click on a dark area of the image that you would like to be the dark point (i.e. the color below which all become black) of the image. The image, and histogram, will be adjusted in line with your change (this is where the "ALT+Comd" to reset can come in really handy).

3. Repeat this step with the Set White Point (rightmost) eyedropper and an area of the image that should be white. In this case, the clock face seems appropriate.

   If you need to zoom in a bit to locate your white point, press CTRL/⌘+SPACE at the same time to temporarily switch to the Zoom tool.

4. If necessary, find a mid-point too. Be careful with this though – only do it if you really think it is needed. It's definitely not necessary on this image.

5. If happy with the results, click OK. Alternatively, you can still make adjustments with the sliders until you are happy.

Our image is definitely a lot better now, though in reality, there might not have been any need to adjust the darker tones. The advantage of this method over the Brightness/Contrast method is that the image retains its sharp contrast, and there is less of a feeling of trade off.

Using the automatic approach can be a little problematic though, depending on whether you can find the appropriate shades in your image. Because this adjusts the red, green, and blue levels separately, it can lead to some pretty strange results. Feel free to look though these histograms, but in a black and white book I think it is safe to say that you'd be better off getting a feel for how they work yourself. They are best used for subtle adjustments when you feel your scanner/camera etc. is picking up red, green and blue unevenly, or for simply looking at the histograms before turning to the overall one.

Auto Levels

The other way of adjusting the levels is so quick it's barely worth mentioning:

1. Open your image.

2. Click Enhance > Auto Levels (or CTRL/⌘+SHIFT +L).

Er... that's it. Although quick and easy, we don't recommend it as it can get fooled by early spikes on the histogram and give strange results.

You can also open the Levels dialog as described in the last section and use the Auto button to see this process at work. This gives you a chance to make your own changes afterwards.

Color casts

An image is affected by a color cast if it unnaturally tends towards a color. The whole image is affected evenly by a color cast, typically because it is something to do with the scanner or digital camera involved.

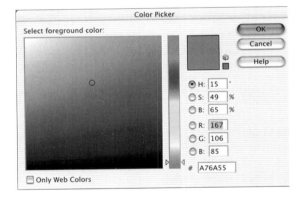

If we throw our minds back to the very start of the book we said a little about color theory. ("What, you skipped that section? It didn't sound very interesting? Well, fair enough..."). We showed you the HSV Color Picker, which works by allowing you to select a hue, then a level of lightness and darkness added to that hue.

Well, as those hues finish right back where they started, they are often represented as a "color wheel", and the color wheel has opposites.

Any picture can be affected by a cast and certain digital cameras are especially prone to this problem. The cast can be in any of the directions (from the center) shown in the wheel, but there cannot be opposite color casts (e.g. blue and yellow) as they would cancel each other out.

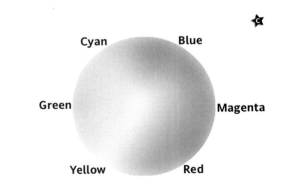

Quick cast removal

If an image is affected by a color cast, it is easy to get rid of so long as your image has areas which should be white or gray.

1. Click Enhance > Adjust Color > Color Cast....

2. Click on an area of your image that should be gray or white, but is affected by the cast.

   The computer will measure how far away the color is from an even shade of white/gray (i.e. one where all three color values, RGB, are equal) and then perform an adjustment to balance that square and adjust all the other pixels the same way. This should remove the cast, but leave the correct color information.

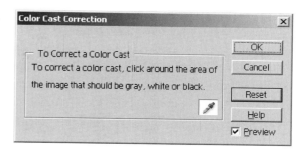

Expert cast removal

In some cases, there is no substitute for using our own eyes to judge this and, mercifully, Photoshop even goes some way to making this easy too (although it used to be slightly easier in the older version).

By clicking Enhance > Adjust Color > Color Variations... we bring up a special dialog that shows us what would happen if we increase or decrease levels of each color.

For reasons best known to Adobe, they have removed the old version, which was based on a color wheel and easier to follow, with this version that thinks only in terms of more or less red, green or blue. By looking at the color wheel we can translate the decreases in red, green or blue into an increase in their opposing color:

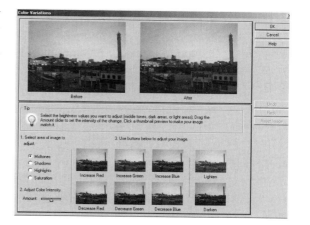

★ Decrease Red = Add Cyan
★ Decrease Green = Add Magenta
★ Decrease Blue = Add Yellow

You can also choose which shades to target your change on using the Midtones/Shadows/Highlights radio buttons to the left. Switching to Saturation is a global change, and does not affect individual color channels.

You can easily remind yourself of this by sliding the Amount slider in the bottom left of the window up a few notches, and watching how the thumbnails change.

The great thing about the Color Variations dialog is that you can keep making changes. For example, if you load an image that veers a long way towards red, and a little way towards blue, you can leave Midtones selected, click a few times on the Decrease Red, and then once on the Decrease Blue preview buttons. All the previews will be updated as you go along.

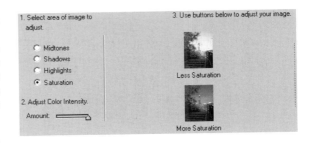

Remember, if you get lost, hold ALT and the Cancel button at the top right of the box temporarily changes to Reset.

Adding a cast with hue and saturation

From time to time, it might be nice to give a photo an "old" look by applying a color cast to it. If we know what color we're going for, then there is no need to be led on a merry dance by the Color Variations dialog. To apply a sepia tone:

1. Open your target image. This effect works a lot better on a photo of something that might look old, unless you're going for an ironic effect.

2. Press CTRL/⌘+U or click Enhance > Adjust Color > Hue/Saturation....

3. Check the Colorize box in the bottom right. If you do not, then the Hue slider moves every pixel of the image along the spectrum, creating some very interesting effects.

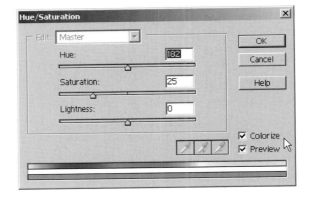

4. The Saturation slider should automatically leap down to about 25. This is a good spot for it.

5. Now drag the Hue slider to about 30 (depending on your view of what sepia is – a contentious issue!). Naturally you can use any color you choose by moving the slider to different points.

6. If the bar at the bottom of your Hue/Saturation dialog looks like a nice solid sepia/brown color, you've got it right. Click OK and your image will be done.

If you have trouble with this, try improving the contrast or levels of your image first.

7. Save your new image with a different name (File > Save As...) so as not to destroy your original colors should you ever need them.

Of course, a sepia tone doth not an old photo make. There are many more tricks in the other chapters of this book that you can use to give your image apparent age. Some of the more obvious include:

★ Adding Film Grain using Filter > Noise > Add Noise.... Selecting Monochromatic is important here, otherwise the noise looks more like bad TV reception!

★ Filter > Texture > Grain can also give good results, depending on the settings.

★ Manual methods can be used to make realistic tears.

★ You could create or use an old-fashioned frame using the Vignette frame in the Effects palette.

More on agimg your photos can be found in Chapter 6, including adding dust/scratches.

Lighting

Another classic photographic problem is poor lighting. Shooting into the sun can often produce little more than a few silhouettes, bad light can make everything seem dull and lifeless. While the levels adjustment is very useful for correcting this sort of effect, there are also some dedicated tools especially designed for this sort of photographic blunder.

Lightening with Fill Flash

While it would be fair to say that nothing can compensate for a complete failure to light your photos, bad results can often be improved using Photoshop. We're going to use this carelessly taken holiday snap in Copenhagen, but the technique applies equally well to indoor shots where the flash has misfired.

1. Open the image that needs correction.

2. If you like, you could perform a Levels adjustment at this stage.

3. Click Enhance > Adjust Lighting > Fill Flash… (or CTRL/⌘+SHIFT+F).

4. Drag the Lighter slider towards the right. This lightens and adds more contrast in all the darker areas of the image, so we have given the Little Mermaid a little more definition, though at the slight expense of lightening the trees in the background too. (A solution would be to use one of the selection tools, see Chapter 2).

5. You may find you need to adjust the Saturation slider a little, as the colors may appear stronger now that they are lighter.

The technique is as simple as that. It won't always work, as you are asking Photoshop to look at a small range of colors and stretch them. That's all well and good, but if that narrow range turns out to be just one or two colors, then there is very little that Photoshop can do. However, that note of caution aside, Fill Flash will work when a flash never could; for instance if you can't get near enough to your subject, or aren't allowed to use it at all.

Backlighting adjustment

Occasionally the problem is reversed. In correctly lighting a subject, you (or your camera's 'auto' function) will often over-expose the background. This is especially true of skies, which often lose their rich colors.

1. Open an image that appears to be bleached by an excessively bright sky or backlight.

2. Click Enhance > Adjust Lighting > Adjust Backlighting....

3. This time the dialog box only has one slider. Adjust it as you see fit. This will make colors, particularly lighter ones, darker

   It's worth bearing in mind that this is an even more hit and miss affair than the Fill Flash, and works far better in conjunction with the selection techniques in *Chapter 2*.

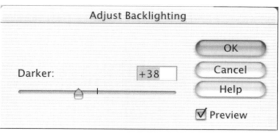

4. Be prepared to give up on this tool if it doesn't appear to be working on your image. If it does, click OK.

The resulting image should have darker, richer skies. The danger is if this happens at the expense of other color ranges used in the picture. In this case, for example, the tree leaves were quite bright, and are now looking slightly strange. Notice also that whites – such as where the sun shines on the tower block to the top left of the photo – remain unaffected. For more control, you are better off using the Levels commands discussed earlier in the chapter.

Recoloring

If deepening the sky just isn't exciting enough for you, you can recolor it altogether. We'll use this worthy but dull picture of Millennium Point, Birmingham. It's already a science museum, so let's give it a weird, futuristic sky.

1. Load your target image, and make any other necessary changes.

2. Click Enhance > Adjust Color > Replace Color…. You will be presented with an unfamiliar dialog box.

3. Ensure that the leftmost eyedropper (just below the word Preview) is selected, then click in the area of the image where you want to change the color.

You will see the thumbnail in the Replace Color dialog change to white. The white areas represent those that are going to be changed in color.

4. Now switch to the middle eyedropper (with a + symbol on it). This will add further ranges of color. You can do this by clicking on areas of your image, or areas of the thumbnail. Continue selecting areas until you're confident that all the areas you wish to affect have changed to white in the thumbnail.

5. If you have accidentally gone over areas you wish you hadn't, either reset the dialog by holding ALT and clicking the Reset button, or select the rightmost eyedropper (with a - symbol on it) and click on areas that you don't want to be affected by the color change.

6. Now turn your attention to the bottom half of the dialog, labeled Transform. Moving the Hue slider changes the color (as if moving around the edge of the color wheel), Saturation increases the richness of that color, and Lightness, well, you're probably there ahead of me...

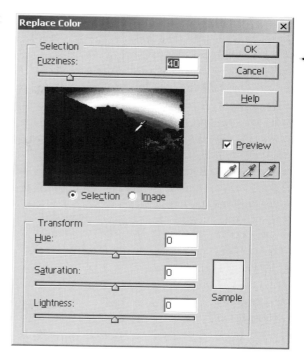

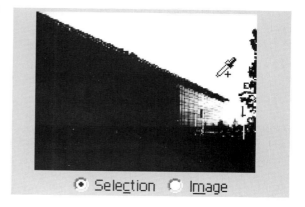

Let's be honest, there aren't too many times that you're going to find yourself creating pink skies, but this tool has other uses. You can use it to recolor all sorts of objects, from clothes and buildings, possibly even to cats!

Focus sharpening

In this chapter we have had a look at a lot of the problems that can affect the whole image. One of the problems that even the best of photographers encounters from time to time is bad focusing. Unlike those magic sequences in Hollywood films where information is found from nowhere in grainy security videos, we're not going to pretend that Photoshop can fix a completely out of focus image. What it can do, though, is sharpen up a slightly fuzzy image.

1. Open your image and make any crops or resolution changes you need to. Anything that changes the resolution, either as part of a crop where you specify a new resolution, or by directly changing the resolution, can add a slight blurring effect to the image, which is why these need to be got out of the way first.

2. Click Filter > Sharpen > Sharpen or, for a stronger effect, Filter > Sharpen > Sharpen More.

The filter that Photoshop applies cannot go back to the time the photo was taken and adjust your lens for you, so instead it increases contrast in areas of the image where there is a change in color, which has the effect of making more defined edges. It only works up to a point (which is why there are only 'Sharpen' and 'Sharpen More' options rather than a whole range and a slider). It is better to under-use this effect than make an image look artificial, which it will quickly do if you try applying the filter more than once.

Selection, copying and manipulation

In this chapter

The last chapter was basically about things that we could do to the whole picture at once; color changes, cropping, levels adjustments, etc. That's all very clever, but we can achieve some of the same blanket effects in the darkroom. In the following pages we'll have a look at how we can use Photoshop to select different areas of images and apply changes only to those areas. In this chapter we'll look at:

★ Using the Marquee tool
★ Using the Lasso tool
★ The Magic Wand
★ Anti-aliasing
★ Feathering
★ The Selection Brush
★ Adding to/removing from selections
★ Copying selections
★ Transforming selections

Basic selection

All the selection tools are grouped together at the top of the Toolbox, and, except the Move and Crop tools, they all have the same function: to single out groups of pixels for alteration. It is the development of these tools that makes modern image editing possible as they bridge the gap between the way we look at pictures, in terms of shapes and objects, and the way the computer does (that grid of pixels described in Chapter 0).

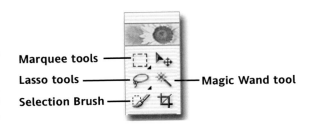

Selection tools all work by drawing a **marquee** around an object. This is a line of slowly moving dots, sometimes called "marching ants" by people in the trade. Everything inside a marquee is selected, everything outside is not, and so any changes only affect the selected area inside the marquee.

All of Photoshop's Selection tools can be used in conjunction with each other, so if we need to select an area that's very different at either end, that's no problem. First, we'll learn how to make a basic selection, then we'll look at how to add and subtract from selections. Then we'll look at some of the more advanced features of selecting objects, like softening or "feathering" the edges.

Selecting an area

Without a doubt, the most intuitive way to select an object is to use one of the Marquee tools. This is because they act in much the same way as selecting a group of files in Windows Explorer or Mac OS Finder – we simply click in one corner of the area we want to select, drag the mouse over our selection, and release the mouse button at the diagonally opposite corner.

1. You can try this now. Load an image, any will do, and use the Marquee tool to select an area of it. For this example we'll be using an image of a phone box.

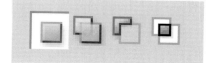

2. Next we need to ensure that the New Selection button in the Options bar (the left-hand button in the image opposite) is pressed. The others are discussed later in this chapter, but they're pretty useful.

3. Now click and hold the mouse button in the start corner, and then drag the mouse to the diagonally opposite corner.

   To select a perfect square (or circle with the Elliptical Marquee tool), we just hold the SHIFT key at the same time.

   To select outwards from the centre point of an area, rather than from the corner, hold the ALT key at the same time (we can even use ALT and SHIFT together).

4. To move our marquee once it's drawn, we can click inside it and drag the whole marquee around without affecting the pixels of the image.

That's pretty much all there is to it. In our example, the only real problem is that our phone box is simply not rectangular!

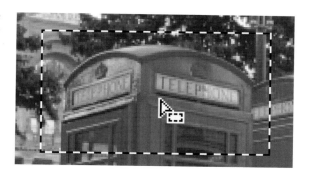

> When an area is highlighted, it can be used for all sorts of things, which are covered in the other chapters. For example, the LEVELS, or the HUE/SATURATION adjustments we looked at in Chapter 1 would only be applied to the selected area if they were used while an area was selected.

Deselecting an area

A concept as important as selecting a marquee is getting rid of it again afterwards. While those little ants are marching along, we can only apply changes to the area of the image that we've got selected. Obviously at some point we'll need to select another area, or none at all.

A tip for when things aren't behaving as expected in Photoshop is to check whether any areas have been left selected by mistake.

Pressing CTRL/⌘+D or clicking Select > Deselect are the easiest ways to completely clear a selection (starting a new one using another Selection tool is possible too). By the same token, we can bring back our most recent marquee by clicking Select > Reselect, or pressing CTRL/⌘+SHIFT+D again.

Selecting complicated shapes

With complicated shapes one possible solution is to make up a selected area from a number of different shapes and mercifully Photoshop makes this very easy indeed. In this example we'll just make two uses of the Marquee tools to select this phone box, but the principles involved can be extended indefinitely.

This is a useful method, and gets pretty quick once we're used to using the keyboard shortcuts.

1. First we ensure nothing is selected by pressing CTRL/⌘+D, and then we select a Marquee tool and pick out the first shape on the image, as we did before.

2. To select the Elliptical Marquee tool we can either switch between rectangular and elliptical at the left of the Options bar (if we're already working with one of these tools) or use the Toolbox.

   When drawing an ellipse, remember to start at the corner of an imaginary rectangle that would contain it, or hold ALT and start from the center.

We can now move our marquee a little if necessary by 'nudging' it with the arrow keys.

3. Once we've drawn our first marquee, we can now change Selection tools if necessary – it will remain selected.

4. To add the new marquee we are going to draw to the previous one, we need to select the Add To Selection button (two overlapping squares) on the Options Bar. The four buttons on the Options Bar appear for each Selection tool.

Each selection tool will remain in the mode it was left in, so it's a good idea to keep an eye on them.

An alternative to using these buttons is to use the keyboard shortcuts. These are:

★ + (add) Hold SHIFT
★ - (subtract) Hold ALT
★ x (intersecting areas only) Hold both SHIFT and ALT.

When selected, they are all indicated by a small symbol drawn at the bottom right of the selection pointer (as in the bottom right of this picture).

5. Finally, we draw a new shape (it can intersect the previous, or not), in this case using the Rectangular Marquee Selection tool. When we release the mouse button, the selection areas will be fused if they intersect. Either way, they now act as one selection, to which further shapes can be added, and effects can be applied, etc.

Inverse selection

A simple trick is to select the opposite area to what we need. For example, if we wanted to select the area around the telephone box, but not the box itself, we could start by selecting the box. There are better ways than using the Marquee tools, but it'll do for the purposes of this demonstration! It's then a simple matter of pressing CTRL/⌘+I or clicking Select > Inverse and Photoshop will simply select all the area that was left out before. We can tell it worked because there is now a row of marching ants at the outside of the window too.

Complicated selection

Selecting simple shapes, or even building up groups is all fairly straightforward, but what about more complicated and random shapes? It would be very difficult to accurately select them using any combination of marquees, so it's quicker to turn to one of the other Selection tools.

> *Remember, any Selection tool can be used to add to or subtract from any other.*

Freehand shape selection

You might think of the Lasso as something best left in Texas, but you'd be wrong, it's a valuable asset in the Photoshop Toolbox too. Despite the name, it doesn't work by throwing ropes, or ants, or anything else as frighteningly difficult as that. In fact, next to the Rectangular Marquee, it's as straightforward as they come. Let's look at an example of the Lasso in use.

1. First, we use the Zoom tool to get close to the object to be selected; this makes accurate use of the Lasso much easier.

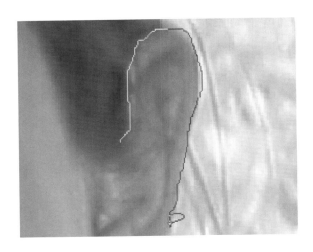

2. Next, click somewhere on the edge of the area to be selected, in our case this ear. It's a good idea to make this first selection at the least defined part of the object, as this will probably be the least smooth part of the mouse pointer's journey.

3. Still holding the mouse, we now move the pointer around the object, drawing a line, which will be the boundary of our selection.

4. When we release the mouse, Photoshop completes the shape by drawing a straight line back to where we started – to minimize how obvious this is, we need to finish as near to the start as possible.

5. If we make any mistakes, we can use the Add To Selection function, as described in the previous example, or the Subtract From Selection button.

To quickly use the Zoom tool, without changing tools in the Toolbox, press CTRL/⌘+SPACE (to zoom in) or ALT+SPACE to zoom out.

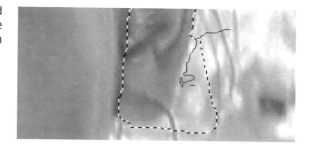

Angular shape selection

If we have a more angular set of shapes, or we're not too bothered about getting a perfect edge to our selection because we're going to do something else to it later, a quicker method is to use the Polygonal Lasso tool, part of the same Toolbox group.

If we were going to remove these ugly tower blocks from behind this canal-side pub, our first step might be to select them. Because of their straight sides, we'll do that using the Polygonal Lasso tool.

★ Two

1. First we select the Polygonal Lasso tool.

2. Then click (and release) the mouse on a corner of the polygon.

3. Now we move to the next point around the shape and click again.

4. We continue to do this around the shape until we get to the corner before the original start point.

5. If we now double click on that last corner, the polygon will be joined up

    OR:

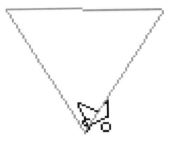

    As we move the mouse near to the original point, an 'O' will appear to the bottom right of the cursor. One click will finish the shape off perfectly.

Automatic shape selection

Looking again at the previous two examples, it would've been handy to just have the computer select the objects, and under certain circumstances, Photoshop can manage this for us. However don't get too excited – it works by trying to spot edges where pixels are of strongly contrasting colors, so it can't make intelligent decisions or identify the edges of all objects.

Using the phone box example image from earlier, we can see how this can work effectively on a clear boundary but become unworkable in other areas.

1. We start by selecting the Magnetic Lasso tool.

2. Then click (and release) somewhere on the outside of the object, and begin to trace the pointer around the edge, following as closely as possible.

3. To make a definite point, especially to mark a corner, click the mouse button once – wherever the line wanders, it will definitely now go via here.

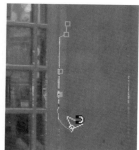

In some areas though, the Magnetic Lasso simply isn't up to it. For example, it won't work well in the gap between the two boxes (which don't look to have been painted too well, while we're paying close attention). We can either click a lot so that the line doesn't have much choice, or just accept it and tidy things up later using one of the other selection tools, or do a bit of both.

4. When we get to the end, the same little 'O' will appear next to the cursor as with the Magnetic Lasso tool. We just need to click once to close off the selection.

OR:

We can double-click elsewhere and Photoshop will try and find contrasting edges on a rough line between the point we double-click and our start point. It goes without saying that this is incredibly hit-and-miss!

Magic Wand

The methods of selection we've seen in the chapter so far are pretty reliant on shapes and edges, but it isn't always the easiest way of doing things, and if you've spent any time playing with the Magnetic Lasso you'll have seen that it isn't always accurate.

The Magic Wand tool works by selecting areas of similar color. There are plenty of adjustments we can make to help Photoshop get these things right and you'll find by using either trial and error or eventually, a practiced eye, that it is one of the easier ways of selecting objects.

A good example of where to use the Magic Wand tool is the clear, boring sky in this Manhattan skyline. Selecting it might be the first step towards removal.

1. We start by selecting the Magic Wand tool.

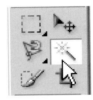

2. Then check that the Options bar is set at its default settings. We've already met the Add, Subtract, and Intersect buttons earlier, and they work just the same for this tool too. Unless we've already selected an area to be part of our selection, we begin by setting it to Add. We also need to consider the tolerance – the higher the tolerance (on a scale of 0 to 255), the wider the range of colors that will be selected. 32 is a good choice.

3. To get the computer to highlight all of the areas of similar color in an image, regardless of whether they're touching or not, we just uncheck the Contiguous button.

4. Then click once somewhere in the area of color we want to select, and a marquee will instantly be drawn around it. In this image, the slight grayness of the clouds towards the right has caused some of our sky to be left out.

5. To select more colors we can use the Add button in the Options bar, or use SHIFT-clicking elsewhere in the image. We can also SHIFT-click somewhere else within the new marquee and select more pixels, as there's a wide range of color shades (the same as the tolerance) represented in it.

Now we have our sky perfectly selected, just ripe for deletion, or color adjustment. Just to try it out, this is the result of setting the tolerance to 50, turning Contiguous off and clicking the Magic Wand in the right-hand end of the sky. Notice all the little areas of the water that have been selected, as they were similar grays to the sky. With the tolerance set to 100, almost all of the lake would be selected as well as the sky.

On an image like this, where the buildings are all very dark anyway, the difference between high and low tolerance isn't apparent, but in other cases it can be a crucial factor. Don't be afraid to deselect a few times and adjust the tolerance until you're happy.

Anti-aliasing

There are a number of ways of selecting objects while at the same time not making the edge too harsh. The marquee boundary is deliberately severe, so we can see it while editing the image, but that isn't likely to be the final effect we're aiming for. For that reason Photoshop lets us make use of a common technique called **Anti-aliasing**.

Anti-aliasing uses shading on the pixels near the edge to create a softer effect. In these two images (scaled up a bit), an area of the sign was selected and then removed. The area underneath was left white. Anti-aliasing was used in the second one, and the difference is obvious.

Most of the time, Anti-aliasing makes an image seem smoother and easier on the eye, which in turn makes it seem more realistic. There are a few circumstances where we might not want to use it though, such as with web graphics where we'll be working with a limited number of colors, or if we're trying to achieve certain other effects. You can either use Anti-aliasing, or not, on any one selection – not half and half.

Feathering

Anti-aliasing essentially mimics the way real life works, softening only pixels that fall on the divide between areas of different shades, in the same way that the eyes only measure from a finite number of points. In a perfect image made up of lines (what computer's call Vector graphics), not pixels, there would be no need for it at all.

However, for photographic images it's a pretty useful effect, and there are some occasions where it would be nice to take it further. For example, we can use it to copy some of the texture surrounding an object, while making it partially transparent. Let's use this image of a boat for an example:

1. First we select an area using one of the Selection tools above (we can also use the Selection Brush tool, which we discuss later in the chapter). In this case we've used the Polygonal Lasso tool to pick up the outline of the boat, and some of the water surrounding it.

2. Next we choose Select > Feather… from the menu or press CTRL/⌘+ALT+D and enter a figure in pixels – the larger the Feather Radius the larger the "halo". We need to use larger figures with higher-resolution images as they use more pixels to represent the same area on the page.

3. The marquee moves to represent the centre point of the feathering (i.e. the point at which the transparency is 50%), which we can now copy/move or alter as we choose.

This final image was created by inverting the selection, by clicking Select > Inverse, and pressing DELETE (to remove the rest of the image). Notice how the feathering has smoothed off the corners. We can achieve a similar smoothing effect without the feathering, by clicking Select > Modify > Smooth….

When using any of the Marquee or Lasso tools, we can choose how much feathering to apply before we select an area. We can do this by typing a value into the box on the Options bar (we just need to remember to check whether there is a feather already set before using the next tool).

Selection Brush tool

A new feature in Photoshop Elements 2 is the Selection Brush tool, which allows us to highlight objects simply by drawing over them. For all of the cleverness of the tools covered earlier in this chapter, this can often seem the most natural and straightforward way to select objects. Another advantage is that we have a range of different brush effects to select from, so we can get soft, hard or even patterned edges.

Advertising ban

A lot of organizations, for one reason or another, try not to advertise other products. Imagine that we wanted to obscure the branding of this bottle of port in a similar manner to those TV companies, with a blurred patch that just fits over the letters. The easiest way would be to select that area and then blur it, but because of the girl's finger, an ellipse would look a bit clumsy. Let's see how we can use the Selection Brush tool to do it better.

If you're following this book through sequentially, then this is the first time we've met any variant of the Brush tool. If you find things are moving a little too fast for you here, take a look at Chapter 6 where painting is covered in detail.

1. We select the Selection Brush tool to start with.

2. Using the Options bar, we next select the size and shape of a brush to suit our needs. To do this we click on the Brush Presets button (which is a wavy line representing the style of the currently selected brush). You can scroll up or down until you find a brush that you like, or use the Brushes drop-down menu to accelerate things a little.

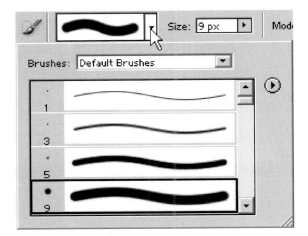

   The size of the brush is measured in pixels, so on a high resolution image, we're affecting less physical area on the final print out than on a lower resolution one. To get an idea of what size we're going to be using, Photoshop turns the pointer into a circle representing the width of the brush head (or uses a crosshair for a very small brush).

3. In this example, we're using a 27 pixel diameter brush with soft (blurry) edges. The soft edges will soften the blow of the blur effect. We've set the Mode menu to Selection.

4. Sometimes it makes things easier if we zoom in closer to the object by pressing and holding CTRL/⌘+SPACE and clicking the mouse.

5. Next, we begin "painting" over the area we want to select using the mouse pointer. A thin marquee will steadily appear around our selection as it forms.

As it is sometimes difficult to see the edges of the selected area, particularly if we're using a soft-edged brush like this one, we can check our progress by switching the mode in the Options bar to Mask. This gives us a good impression of our progress (showing everywhere unaffected by our selection as red). Just remember to switch back afterwards!

6. Once we've finished our selection, we are free to apply whatever effect we wish to it. In this case, we've gone for the classic pixilation effect by clicking Filter > Pixelate > Mosaic. Because we chose the soft-brush, there are areas where the mosaic squares also have bits of detail showing from underneath, which looks a little better than if the area had harsh edges.

Moving and copying

So far, we've seen a few changes applied to selected areas of an image. Another thing we can do to our selections is to move them around, or even distort them.

Moving selections

In this example, we're going to move a simple shape: this red ball.

1. We'll start by selecting the object (here we used the Magic Wand tool with a few additional SHIFT-clicks at different color shades).

2. Next, we select the Move tool (or simply begin to drag our object while using any Selection tool except the Selection Brush). Either way, click and hold anywhere within your selection. The pointer should change to a small black arrow as pictured.

3. We can now drag the selection around, and release the mouse button when we're happy with the object's new position.

> *The area formerly occupied by the object is replaced with whatever the currently selected background color is.*

Copying selections

Using the same red ball from the last example, we'll now see how to copy a selection.

1. As before, we start by selecting the object we wish to copy using an appropriate selection tool.

2. Then we select the Move tool and move the mouse pointer over our selection.

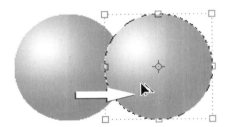

3. If we hold down the ALT key while the mouse pointer is still over the selection, it gets a shadow. We can now click and drag the object to another location and a copy of the original will remain.

4. We can repeat this process as often as we like (the most recent clone, which appears to be nearest you, remains selected at the end of a copy).

Transforming selections

If you tried the above example, the keen eyed amongst you will surely have spotted the square "handles" around the selected object. This is part of what is known as the Free Transform tool, and can also be accessed by selecting an object and pressing CTRL/⌘+T or Image > Transform > Free Transform.

It's a way of manipulating the selected pixels as if they were a real shape, allowing us to create all sorts of effects – from Pinocchio noses to everything else in the hall of mirrors. The only word of caution is that, because we're working with pixels, there is only a finite amount of data we can work with and every time we accept a set of changes, we lose some of our original information. If we make the object a lot larger, then that process is all the more exaggerated. Let's demonstrate this point by giving this man, who's looking just a little too smug at the moment, comically big Dumbo-ears.

1. As usual we start by selecting the target area. In this example, we've selected the ear using the Magnetic Lasso. Then we expand the selection slightly using the Select > Modify > Expand feature which simply redraws the selection one (or however many we choose) pixel(s) bigger all around. This is just to ensure we're catching all of the ear.

When expanding a shape away from its original home, it's best to select an appropriate background color – in this case black.

2. Next, click Image > Transform > Free Transform or press CTRL/⌘+T and editing handles (the squares) will appear around the selection.

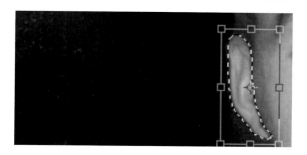

3. Now we can adjust the shape to our heart's content. You may have noticed that as we move the pointer over the different handles, it changes to represent the effect it would have if the mouse were clicked. These effects are:

    ★ **Scaling**. We can scale the image by dragging any of the squares on the bounding box. As before, holding down SHIFT while dragging the mouse scales proportionally to the selection's dimensions.

    ★ **Rotational**. When the pointer is outside the image it becomes a curved arrow, and clicking allows us to rotate the image.

    ★ **Movement**. If we move the pointer inside the selection it changes to a small black arrow, and can be used to drag it around.

    ★ **Single-corner movement** can be achieved by holding down SHIFT as we move the corners.

    While we are adjusting our image, it will be represented by a lower quality "preview", which can be quickly redrawn by Photoshop.

4. When we're finally happy with the image, we can just click on the Commit except tick (or press ENTER) on the Tool Options bar to commit the changes. It's only now that Photoshop actually performs the complicated work of making the final image.

There are still "quality issues" in this example because we scaled up dramatically from a smaller ear (to prove a point), but it is a definite improvement! The trick is not to blow objects up too dramatically, or to always work with a very high-resolution, sharply focused original. We've blown this ear up by about 300% (width ways, at least) so we should have started at 900dpi (which would be 300 when blown up), rather than a slightly blurred 300dpi.

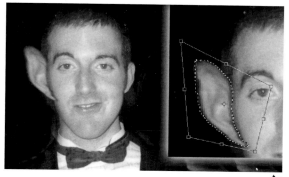

Perspective

All that free transforming above is a lot of fun, but there's more than a slight danger of getting carried away. To perform a similar range of effects, but in a slightly more controlled environment, we can access Skewing, Distortion, and Perspective effects separately from the Image > Transform > menu. In the case of Perspective, this is especially handy as Photoshop helps judge the scales for us.

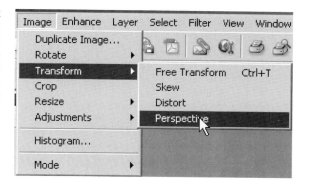

Using the Perspective tool, the corner handles (squares) now affect each other so here, in our "boring shape", where the top-right corner has been brought in, the top-left one automatically followed by an equal amount.

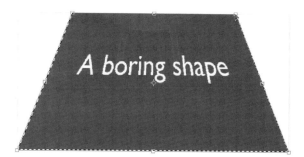

★ Two

To achieve a sideways perspective, we can hold the pointer over the bounding box at the top-center and drag it sideways. Our selected area is now scaled to imply either perspective, or that it is itself a shadow.

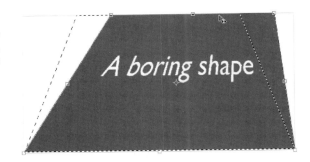

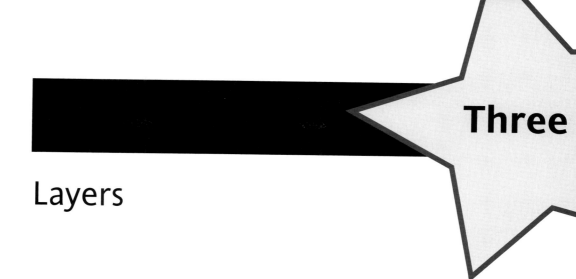

Three

Layers

In this chapter

Playing with the selection tools it becomes quickly apparent that we'll have problems if they're the only way of editing images. Luckily, they're just the beginning. In this chapter we'll introduce and explore the concept of layers – perhaps the most powerful single aspect of Photoshop (if they can be considered a single aspect in any way).

In short, layers allow us to break an image into parts and move things around to suit – the basis of a montage, for example. The longer version is, well, a little more complex than that, and in fact forms the rest of this chapter. This is what we'll be covering:

- ★ The Layers palette
- ★ Creating layers
- ★ Moving and duplicating layers
- ★ Linking and merging layers
- ★ Transparency
- ★ Adjustment layers
- ★ Layer masks
- ★ Layer management
- ★ Flattening images
- ★ Saving and exporting
- ★ Blending modes
- ★ Layer styles

Theory

There is a lot to think about with layers, and it can be a little daunting, but in reality their appeal is their simplicity. Traditional animators have understood the logic behind them for many years – an image is easier to work on, and more versatile, if you don't have to redraw from scratch all the time.

A traditional animator would have used layers on "BOB" here to do things like redraw some parts of him for different frames of animation. In this case, we've drawn the layers, from top down, as:

- ★ Hat
- ★ Features
- ★ Legs
- ★ Body
- ★ Background

Admittedly, the background isn't much to write home about (it's just white) but the other layers are all transparent where nothing has been added.

A traditional animator would see something like this: four sheets of acetate arranged one above the other (over a white work surface, let's say). Each of these sheets could be moved around separately, or one could be removed altogether. In Photoshop, we aren't animating anything, and there's no acetate, but the principle of the Layers palette is much the same.

So the big difference between animation acetate and Photoshop layers is what it's used for. In Photoshop (most of the time at least) we're not animating anything. We just want to make our life easier, and ensure that we can change our minds later if we're unhappy with the result. This is something often referred to as **non-destructive editing** and layers are very useful for it as they can be built up, copied and adjusted at any time.

The other principal difference is how much more we can do than an animator with acetate; we can adjust our layers' opacity, add shadows, glows and other effects to our layers, hide them, group them, and apply special adjustments to them.

In fact a really simple little trick would be to give our friend "Bob" here a shadow; by making a copy of the layer(s) he's on, then applying a perspective, and perhaps even a blur effect. We could then make the shadow partially see-through, so it appeared over whatever background we chose to put underneath. The list goes on....

Layers are only fully preserved by saving the file in the default PSD (Photoshop) format. Until we're certain we've finished all work on our creation, we need to keep a copy in this format.

Introduction to the Layers palette

As we've already seen, Photoshop is in the habit of replacing a traditional approach to artwork of some kind with one of its palettes. The Layers palette can be thought of as the equivalent of the animator's peg-board (which he/she uses to line up the acetate cells under the camera). Let's take a closer look, to get a handle on it. The first step is to drag the Layers palette from the Palette Well at the top of the screen. It's sometimes handy to tuck the Layer Styles palette behind this one, but you may prefer to leave it where it is for now.

★ Three

The following image points out what all the parts of the Layers palette are or do:

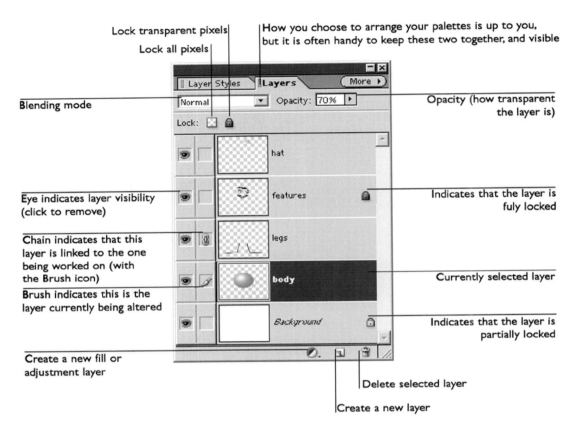

Lock transparent pixels

Lock all pixels

How you choose to arrange your palettes is up to you, but it is often handy to keep these two together, and visible

Blending mode

Opacity (how transparent the layer is)

Eye indicates layer visibility (click to remove)

Indicates that the layer is fully locked

Chain indicates that this layer is linked to the one being worked on (with the Brush icon)

Brush indicates this is the layer currently being altered

Currently selected layer

Indicates that the layer is partially locked

Create a new fill or adjustment layer

Delete selected layer

Create a new layer

A close look at the Layers palette can be pretty frightening at first, but in reality it's pretty simple. It is built around its core purpose – the layers, which are represented by thumbnail images of their contents and their names. (Naming your layers isn't essential, as Photoshop will assign them one like Layer 1 automatically but it is a good habit to get into, especially on complicated projects.)

To the left of each layer's thumbnail there are also two icons. The leftmost, the "eye", represents whether the layer is currently visible, and the rightmost shows its status. We can click on the layer visibility icon to hide it, which can sometimes make other layers easier to work on.

If we click a layer thumbnail or it's name, the status icon will change to a "brush" symbol to show that it's the active layer. Photoshop can also automatically select the active layer for us. If, for example, we select the Text tool, and then click somewhere on the page where there is already some text, Photoshop switches to that layer and makes it the live layer.

If we clicking on any of the empty squares in that second column, this will cause the "chain link" icon to appear. This means that layer is linked to the currently selected layer (the one with the "brush" icon). Once linked, all of these layers will be selected at the same time should any of them be selected. So, for example, they will move together if the Move tool is used. Clicking the "chain link" icon again will unlink it. Obviously we cannot deselect the "brush" icon like this, as we can't unlink a layer from itself.

Customizing the palette

It might not be the first question in your mind, but it's worth knowing that we can customize the Layers palette to suit the size of our monitor, or your eyesight! Let's see how:

1. Click on the More button at the top right of the Layers palette and select Palette Options… from the bottom of the menu.

2. Now, just select the thumbnail size that suits us best. However, while bigger thumbnails are very useful, they also reduce the number of layers that we can see in a vertical direction as they are taller.

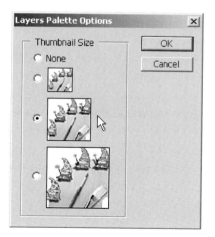

Creating new layers

Once you're happy with the appearance of your Layers palette, it's time to actually have some layers to work with. There are four main ways to create layers:

- ★ We can click on the Create a new layer button (the middle one) at the bottom right-hand corner of the palette.

- ★ We can select Layer > New > Layer... from the Menu bar.

- ★ We can simply press CTRL/⌘+SHIFT+N.

- ★ Or finally, we can use the Layers palette More menu.

Every technique except the "new layer" button on the palette launches the New Layer dialog box, which gives us a chance to name it. However, pressing ALT as we click the "new layer" button brings up the dialog. Essentially, we're just making a convenience decision.

We'll discuss the Mode and Opacity options of the New Layer dialog later, but these work in exactly the same way as the buttons on the Layers palette.

New layers are placed directly above the active (highlighted) layer, not necessarily on the top, and will become the active layer as soon as they are created.

Moving layers

Once you've got a few layers, there is a fair chance that you're going to want to start moving them around. That's also fairly easily achieved (if you've got nothing to work with, you can access the example file here, called `chapter03eg02.psd` in the download). In the example image there are three layers; a black edged white square layer, which is above a colored circle layer, on top of a white background layer. As an example, let's move the square layer behind the circle layer:

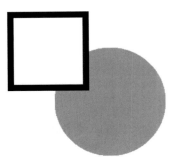

1. First, click on the name or thumbnail (in the Layers palette) of the layer to be moved and hold down the mouse button.

2. Then drag the layer up or down the palette. As we move the gray rectangle outline, which represents the layer, over the other layers, a black bar indicates where the layer will fall if we release the mouse.

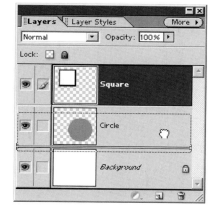

3. When that bar is in the correct place, we just release the pointer. If there are more layers than can be seen in the palette, it will scroll automatically if we drag the gray outline past the top or bottom.

   A word of advice; be careful not to release the gray outline over any of the buttons at the bottom of the Layers palette by mistake, or you could find it deleted!

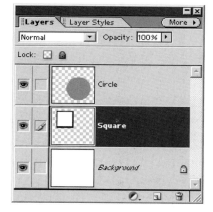

4. After you've dropped the layer in its new position, Photoshop will instantly update the image to reflect the changes.

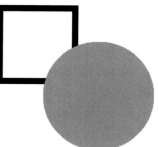

Duplicating layers

If, for some reason, we wanted another identical layer to work with it'd be a shame to have to redraw it; luckily we don't have to! For this example, let's say that we need two similar squares:

1. We can simply duplicate the layer using any of these three methods:

   ★ Drag the layer (as if copying) and release it on the New Layer button at the bottom of the screen. As before, if we hold down ALT we get a chance to name the layer.

   ★ Make the layer active (by clicking once in the Layers palette) and use the More menu's Duplicate Layer... option.

   ★ Make the layer active and use the Layer > Duplicate Layer... menu option.

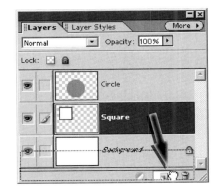

2. That's actually all there is to duplicating layers, but it isn't a lot of good on its own, as the copy appears exactly in front of itself. To move it, we just select the Move tool from the Toolbox.

3. Now we can click on and drag our new shape or, if we don't want to move it far, click on the layer's name in the palette and move it gently using the arrow keys to nudge it one pixel at a time.

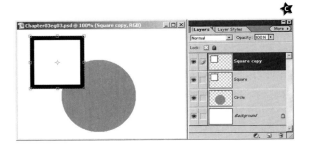

4. Finally, we could even rotate the shape a little, to give a jauntier, less regimented feel. Other transform options are available much as with what we've seen already.

Linking and merging layers

The picture we've just created in the last section (chapter03eg03.psd) looks a little like a pair of uncomfortable glasses on a giant red nose. Well, it does if you squint! However, if they were glasses, they ought to act in unison, not be on two separate layers. Let's have a look at how we can get them to act as one:

1. First, we select either the copied layer or the original, and then link the two by clicking in the empty box in the other layer. When we do this, a "chain link" icon will appear, showing that the layer is linked.

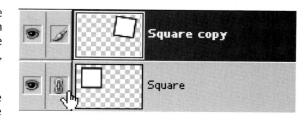

   The two layers will now act together for the purposes of some of the tools, for instance the Move tool, but are still separate layers. To make them truly one, we must perform, another step.

2. To merge the layers we click More> Merge Linked in the Layers palette, or Layer > Merge Linked from the Menu Bar, which will create one layer from the two. If the images overlap, any pixels on the higher layer(s) outweigh those on the lower layer(s).

The thumbnail says it all! Notice that the name of the layer that was active (darker) at the time we merged layers is retained.

Transparency

The last of the "layer basics" might be considered to be the transparency feature which, now we're comfortable with the basics, is worth playing with.

If those squares represent glasses, and it's a big if, then they should at least be see through! Let's see how to do this:

1. Select the newly-merged Square copy layer (or any layer you want to alter the opacity of).

2. Next, click on the small arrow icon next to the Opacity percentage at the top of the Layers palette.

3. Then simply use the tiny slider that appears to choose a new Opacity value, with 0% being complete transparency. We can alternatively just type a new opacity percentage into the box. The results are instant, and can be changed again whenever we like.

It's easy to see the effect we've had – where the black lines were over the white background, they're now a 50% gray. By the same token, bits of the red nose are now visible as pink segments in the white areas of the "glasses". Unfortunately we've now got gray rims instead of black, so this isn't a perfect solution to our problem – there will be one later in the chapter.

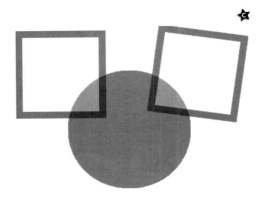

For now though, that is about it for the basics of layers – we've just covered all the basic concepts. Now we need to see some areas in a little more detail.

Adjustment layers

In Chapter 1 there are a number of pictures that we make quick and simple changes to; levels, hue/saturation, and the like. In keeping with the spirit of non-destructive editing, we can use layers toreplicate these effects without permanently affecting the pixels underneath.

This picture of some boats sailing on the River Thames, for example, is suffering from a real shortage of contrast, but if we're unsure of the best way forward, we could try some **Adjustment Layers** without damaging our original. Let's try it out:

1. First, we open an image, from our camera/scanner, etc.

2. Notice how the only layer is called Background by default. Next we click on the 'Create New Adjustment Layer' (the circle) button at the bottom of the Layers palette.

3. Much as with the overall changes in Chapter 1, we click Levels... to open the Levels panel.

4. Now we perform whatever levels adjustment we need to (for advice, refer back to Chapter 1). In this example, the eyedroppers were used, and clicked on a lighter area of the sky, so that the clouds became very white.

5. After making our adjustments and clicking OK, we're returned to the Layers palette, with a new layer. A few items have been added here which are new:

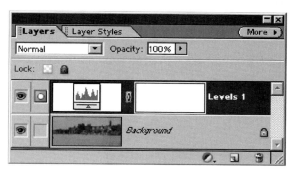

★ In place of the "brush" icon, we have an icon indicating that this is a mask.

★ In place of the image thumbnail, is a mini-histogram. This is in fact an icon representing the fact that this is a levels adjustment layer.

★ A small link icon.

★ A mask thumbnail. This white area is in fact a thumbnail representing a mask of the layer, which is automatically created (see following page). The fact it is completely white is because the whole layer is affected by the adjustment layer.

Layer masks

Continuing from the previous example, our levels adjustment has been quite successful, but we've really brought out the pink of the sailing boats a little too much. The solution is to apply an adjustment layer to them locally, using a mask. A mask in Photoshop is like a mask in painting or stenciling – it's used to stop ink (or effects) going through in places:

1. We begin by creating a new adjustment layer, as before, but this time choose Hue/Saturation..., and set the saturation down by about 25 points (so the sails are visibly deepened in color).

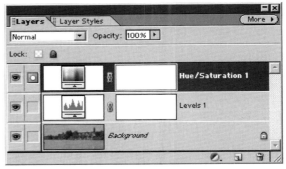

2. Keeping the Hue/Saturation layer active, we need to select the sails using the Magic Wand tool, and give it a high tolerance – about 60 – as well as turning off the Contiguous function on the Options bar. We can get away with this as the pink is such a different color to the rest of the image.

3. To be sure of getting all of the sails, click Select > Modify > Expand..., then Select > Feather..., both with radii of about 2.

4. Next we click Select > Inverse to reverse the selection, and make everything but the sails selected.

5. Ensuring the currently selected background color is black (and still on the Hue/Saturation layer), press the Delete key (or click Edit > Cut).

The result of this is to create a mask where most of the original active areas (white) had been deleted (replaced with black), so that the only remaining active areas are over the sails. This means we can now decide how bright we want the sails individually, without affecting the rest of the image, by double-clicking on the Hue/Saturation logo (to the left of the mask thumbnail) and changing our Hue/Saturation settings.

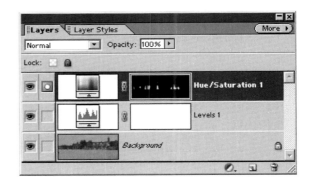

> *To project the mask onto the main picture-editing window, press ALT+Click on the thumbnail in the Layers palette. In effect, the white areas represent 100% opacity, the black 0%, and the gray levels in-between.*

Masking shortcut keys

Here are some useful key-presses when using the masking:

★ SHIFT+ALT+Click on the thumbnail to make a red, transparent version of the mask appear over your image.

★ CTRL/⌘+Click to select those areas of the mask above 50% gray (that is, the white bits).

★ SHIFT+Click the mask to turn it off – a red cross will appear over the mask, and the adjustment layer will now apply to the whole image.

Other adjustment layers

Just for the record, here's a list and description of all the useful adjustment layers. They are:

★ Solid Color..., which creates a layer of the currently selected foreground color. We can use this to tint objects or areas using the opacity settings and the mask.

★ Gradient..., is similar to Solid Color..., but provides a graduated shade – handy for simulating a filter.

★ Levels..., histogram control on the contrast.

★ Brightness/Contrast..., this is more intuitive, but less in-depth, contrast control.

★ Hue/Saturation..., can be used for a variety of purposes, from toning down pink sails (see above) to colorizing an image.

★ Invert, – a negative effect.

★ Threshold... use the histogram to select a point; everything lighter will become white, everything below black, a bit like a bad photocopy.

★ Posterize…, select a number of colors and the image will be reduced to that number – can have some interesting effects.

All of these styles can be used with masks and adjustable levels of opacity.

Layer management

The basics and some uses of layers are discussed above. After exploring the effects that can be created with layers, you'll soon find yourself using lots of them in your images. Given the virtually limitless number of layers that we can use, it's well worth developing a consistent approach to using them. Without meaning to be too prescriptive, this little section is as much about what you can do for Photoshop as what Photoshop can do for you!

Naming layers

This is very worthy, but quite boring, so we won't dwell for long. Simply, we can double-click on the name of a layer in the Layers palette to change it.

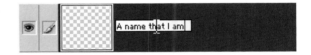

Background layer

There is always a Background layer when we start editing an image. By default, this is partially locked, which means, in essence that we can't make a hole in it! When we edit an ordinary layer, and use the Eraser tool (or any other means of removing pixels), it simply punches a hole through so we can see the layer below.

In a layer that has been partially locked (that is the transparent pixels fixed) we can only change the color of pixels that have color already. If we try and erase over a colored pixel, it will change to the current background color, but not vanish. If we try and erase the transparent areas nothing will happen, and with partially transparent pixels, we can affect their tint, but their degree of transparency remains the same.

The Background layer behaves in just this way, and doesn't start with any transparent pixels. We cannot adjust its setting (the 'Lock' buttons are grayed-out when it is the active layer). We *can* create a transparent layer, then delete the background underneath, but look out for problems when exporting – not all other software can understand transparency in the same way as Photoshop.

> A handy tip is to immediately duplicate the background of any image you start working on so you've always got quick access to a backup.

Adjusting individual layers

In previous examples, we've seen how it's possible to link layers by means of the chain icons, and to use adjustment layers with masks to alter our images in part or in whole. So far, though, (masking aside) adjustment layers have had to apply to the whole image, which isn't always the easiest way of doing things. One of the things about montage is that we often have different images taken under different lighting conditions, but want to be able to balance them perfectly.

Hard as it may be to believe, these two characters weren't sat next to each other when their photographs were taken – they are on separate layers, with their different backgrounds erased to be transparent.

In order to make them look a little more believable, we need to apply levels adjustments to the layers individually:

1. We start by selecting the level that we would like to be adjustable, so that it becomes the active layer, in this case the layer containing the man with the glasses.

2. Next we click Layer > New Adjustment Layer > Levels... from the main menu, and then check the Group With Previous Layer button in the New Layer dialog. By grouping a layer to another it only acts on that layer immediately beneath it, as opposed to all those below it.

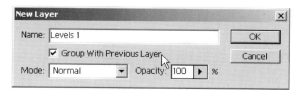

3. We then make our levels adjustment; which will only affect the layer that we selected.

4. After we click OK, this new layer will be represented in the Layers palette above its target layer, with an arrow pointing towards the target layer's thumbnail.

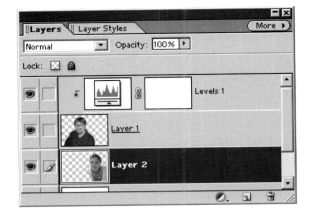

We can also group a layer after it has already been created by selecting it, dragging it just above the target layer in the Layers palette and clicking CTRL/⌘+G (Layer > Group with Previous).

More on using this technique is included in Chapter 4.

Flattening images

While working in layers is undoubtedly very useful, it is also a very memory-hungry way of working. Pixels require memory, which are a finite resource in any computer, so it's often necessary to merge layers. Merging linked layers is covered earlier in this chapter, but there are other ways to do it, like through the Layers palette More button:

★ Merge Down: this command merges the active layer with the layer immediately below it. Simple but effective.

★ Merge Visible: this command makes life very easy when we are using layers to preview effects and how they act with each other. Here, for example, the Posterize effect layer has been made invisible by clicking on the "eye" to its left. Happy with the result, we can click Merge Visible, although we must ensure that one of the visible layers is active when we do.

★ Flatten Image: this reduces the entire image to one layer, so we have to be pretty confident before doing this (or have a backup of a layered PSD saved).

Saving and exporting

When you come to save a file, Photoshop will save the layers by default if you save a Photoshop (PSD) file. This means that next time you come back to your masterpiece, you'll be able to pick up where you left off. You can turn off Layers in the Save Options (pictured) but Photoshop will make it clear that you'll lose information. Why would you want to? Because flattened images make for smaller files, better suited to exporting to other programs, like e-mail, or a word processor, for example.

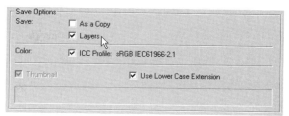

If you're exporting an image to another program, you're unlikely to need layer information, as you aren't going to be able to edit your image in that other program. Equally, if you are e-mailing it to show someone, keeping the size down is the most important thing. Let's take a look at saving images in different formats:

1. First, click File > Save As... (The "Save As" command, in many programs, is a way of saving a file we are already working on in a different place, leaving us with two copies).

2. Next, select an appropriate format for export. You'll probably have a better idea of what you want, depending on your circumstances, but if in doubt, select JPEG from the pull-down menu – this is a common, and very small (high-compression) internet format ideally suited for sending pictures via e-mail.

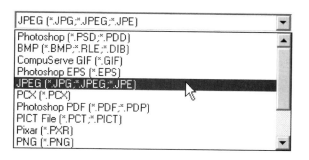

If we select JPEG format, the Layers option ceases to be available, as it's not able to handle layers. In fact very few other formats are able to, except TIFF, but even then not many programs that can read TIFFs can read the layers that Photoshop saves.

3. The Save As dialog will present some other choices, depending on the selected file format. Do this as you think fit – if you are saving a TIFF, you'll be given another chance to think about layers!

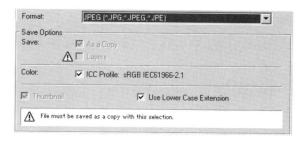

Blending Modes

Earlier in this chapter we tried to pretend that two squares and a circle were actually a face with "glasses", and then made the glasses slightly transparent. The only problem was that this also made the glasses frames transparent too. This is because we were thinking in a narrow way and only adjusting the opacity of our entire layer.

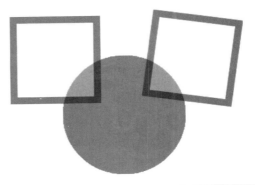

By using **Blending Modes**, we can alter the way the layers interact with each other, and so affect the final image. We'll do this here by sticking the "nose" back on top of the squares layer, then changing the top layer's Blending Mode using the pull-down menu.

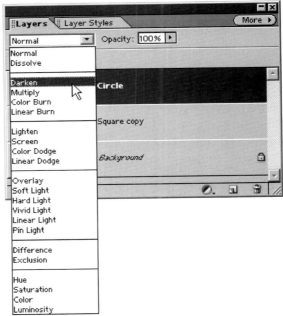

For example, if we change it to Darken the result is that, although the circle is on top (and so appears visible through the "glasses") it is darkened by the layer beneath it. As the squares are black, they're naturally darker than the red circle on top, so they 'blend' through.

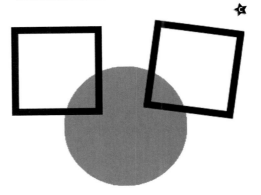

Blending Mode effects

Many, many Photoshop users never even consider playing with blending modes, which is understandable, as they're about as complicated as layers – already a tricky concept – can get. To be honest, they're quite easy to forget about too. That said; they do have some very practical uses that might not be immediately apparent from the above example.

A common use is in altering the "feel" of an image – you can try it by opening an image, duplicating the background layer by dragging it onto the 'New Layer' icon, and then trying out some of the different blending modes. Remember that you can also increase or decrease the strength of the effect by using the Opacity slider.

It isn't easy to convey the likely outcome of all this experimentation in print, yet the greatest crime of an instructional guide is to say "well, here are the buttons, have a play", so here is a quick run down of the blending modes.

Using this demonstration image, we'll have a quick look at all the blending modes – and this will be repeated in the color section because, let's be honest, the spectrum isn't all that obvious here, is it? The different blending modes will only be applied to the top layer, Background copy 2, each time. This file is included in the book download on the friendsofed.com web site, so you can try it yourself.

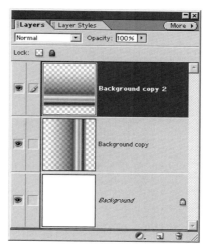

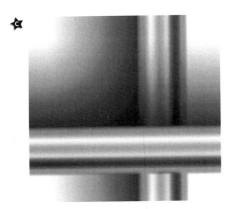

Normal: The default setting, with "normal" blending, meaning colors overlay each other and where there is transparency, the overlaid color only affects the color beneath to the extent of its opacity.

Dissolve: Makes the layer it is applied to "grainy" Pixels take on solid colors, or total transparency.

Darken: Chooses whichever is the darkest pixel of the active layer or what lies beneath. Note the effect where the spectrums cross.

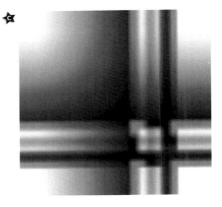

Multiply: Gives a darker effect by "multiplying" the pixels being applied to each other, so that a color x white = the same, but a color x black = black.

Color Burn: Darkens the color of the active layer in proportion to the darkness of the color beneath. Where the color underneath is white, no color shows up.

Linear Burn: Darkens the color underneath to reflect the active layer, so it stays the same on white.

Lighten: Selects whichever pixel of the active or underlying layers is lightest.

Screen: According to the guide "Looks at each channel's color information and multiplies the inverse of the blend and base colors". There's a mouthfull! The effect is to lighten the active layer, especially where the one beneath is light.

Color Dodge: Brightens the underlying image with the color of the active layer, which in this instance has quite a nice haphazard effect as the underlying grays get lighter towards the left of the example image.

Linear Dodge: Like the linear burn, this works the other way to the Color Dodge, instead brightening the image to reflect the active layer by adjusting brightness, giving a lighter, softer effect.

Overlay: A combination of Multiply and Screen modes, depending on the underlying colors. It darkens dark areas and lightens the light.

Soft Light: An altogether more pleasing approach, with similar results to the Overlay, but using a combination of Dodge and Burn modes to give a spotlight-like effect, so much less extreme.

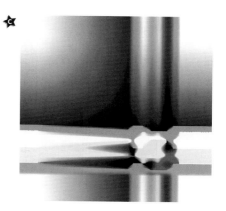

Hard Light: Much more like a brighter light, this works like the Overlay function but takes its cue from the top layer, not the image beneath.

Vivid Light: Treats the active layer as a light source, and Burns or Dodges the below image's contrast depending on how light they are.

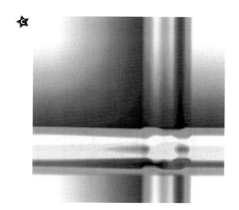

Linear Light: Works like Vivid Light, but creates a smoother result as it doesn't exaggerate contrast.

Pin Light: Replaces colors darker than the active layer with colors from the active layer.

Difference: Subtracts whichever pixel has the highest brightness value, the effect being this psychedelic inversion.

Exclusion: Produces a similarly mathematical result to Difference, but with reduced contrast.

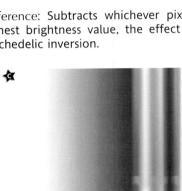

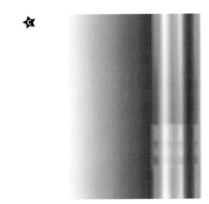

Hue: Tints the lower layers with its color shade, but only where they already have a color value themselves.

Saturation: The saturation level of the layer is applied to lower ones – that is the brighter the layer, the more saturated the one below.

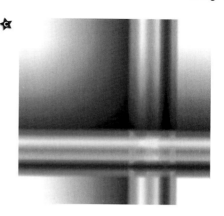

Color: The color and saturation levels of the active layer are applied to those below it.

Luminosity: Applies the grayscale value of the active layer to those beneath it.

The number and variety of these Blending Modes can be more than a little daunting, but it is definitely worth experimenting. If it doesn't work, you can always undo (CTRL/⌘+Z), or delete your layer by dragging it to the bin in the bottom right of the palette. Each layer can only have the one mode applied to it, but you can stack them up.

Layer Styles

Blending Modes are a little complicated, there is no getting away from that, and a little perseverance might be required to get used to them straight away. **Layer Styles**, on the other hand, are a quick and simple way of coming up with an effect.

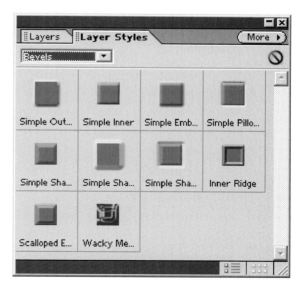

Photoshop 7, the grand master of image editing software, has a very complicated, very flexible approach to layer styles. Adobe has managed to retain a lot of that flexibility In Photoshop Elements 2, while also providing us with this handy palette to make things a little easier.

After the Layers palette, you'll be pleased to hear that there is nothing so complex here. The two buttons at the bottom right simply switch between this thumbnail view and a list layout, whichever you prefer. The other important points are the drop-down menu to the top left, and the round 'clear style' icon just beneath the More button.

Preset styles

Let's start with a simple image, of a hexagon and a square, chapter03eg07.psd in the download.

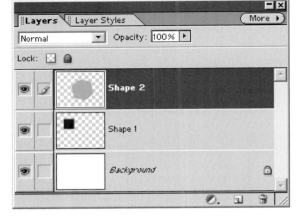

1. First, we select Shape 1 (or whatever layer the target object is on). It must be surrounded by transparency for Layer Styles to work.

2. Then open up the Layer Styles palette.

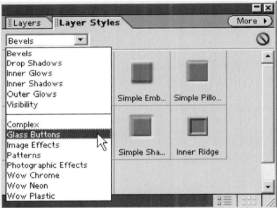

3. Next, we use the drop-down menu to select one of the preset styles – these are the ones in the second half of the menu. Some below the Complex button are quite exciting, but for this example, we'll use Glass Buttons.

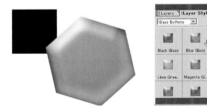

4. We next just choose one of the thumbnails that takes our fancy and click on it. The layer will instantly be redrawn to reflect the change.

That really is all there is to it. Now, when we return to the Layers palette a new "F" logo has appeared to the right of the layer we applied the style to, but there is no evidence of the changes on the layer thumbnail.

Classic styles

All of the styles in the top half of the drop-down menu can be used in conjunction with each other (one from within each sub-set), and they are a little more straightforward. Let's continue with our example:

1. First we'll bring the square layer to the front (drag it to the top of the palette).

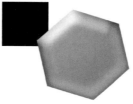

2. Next, ensuring that the Shape 1 (square) layer is the active, we can switch to the Layer Styles palette, and select Bevels from the drop-down menu.

3. If it helps you to find styles, change the view by clicking the List button on the bottom right, then for this example select the Simple Sharp Outer style.

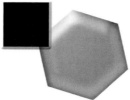

4. Following on, we switch back to the Layers palette and double-click on the "F" icon on the Shape 1 (square) layer.

5. We can now adjust the size of the bevel around our shape by dragging the Bevel Size slider.

Different parts of the Style Settings dialog will become available depending on which layer style we apply. If we were applying a shadow, for example, we could drag the clock-like Lighting Angle dial around and the shadow will be applied in different directions.

Removing styles

It's not always that obvious, but to remove any styles that we've applied, we need to click on the Clear Styles icon, which is always at the top right of the Layer Styles palette. This will remove all the styles we've applied and leave the objects visible as before. We can stop this happening by simplifying (rasterizing) the layer from the Layer palette More menu, but this will lose all the old pixels under the layer style(s) we've added.

Cartoon time

Just to round off what has been a long and technical chapter, lets have a little fun. We'll take our friend from the first few pages, who we promised never to meet again (sorry folks), and get him to move. We won't get over ambitious, as Photoshop isn't exactly an animation studio, but perhaps he could give us a wave?

1. Open the Bob image from your download and then flatten all the layers by clicking Flatten Image from the More menu in the Layers palette.

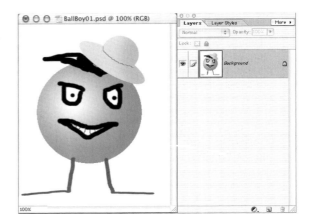

2. Next, we'll draw on some nice arms, which can be seen in the image thumbnail. A detailed discussion of painting techniques is included in Chapter 6.

3. Next, we need to copy the original layer by clicking Duplicate Layer... from the More menu in Layers palette.

4. Now, we'll make some changes to our image in the newly created layer – you will still see the other layer below, but don't worry too much about that.

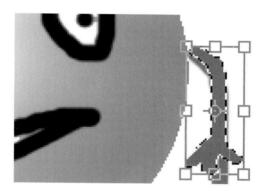

> A tip is to reduce the opacity of all the layers while working on them. This emulates a professional technique called "onion-skinning", whereby animation frames are drawn on transparent sheets above copies of the previous frame.

5. Repeat this process of copying a layer and changing it with as many layers as you like to create frames of animation. Remember, you can draw what you like on each, but if you make small changes you'll get a better animated effect.

The background layer is considered the first frame of animation, and any on top, the subsequent ones. If a program cannot play animated GIFs, it will display that first frame.

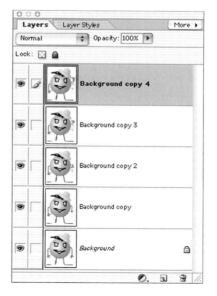

If you want to create an animation that cycles back and forwards, create all the frames for something to move in one direction, then copy all of them except the last one in the opposite order.

6. The next thing to do to create our animated GIF is to click File > Save for Web.... The following image shows the options the Save For Web dialog.

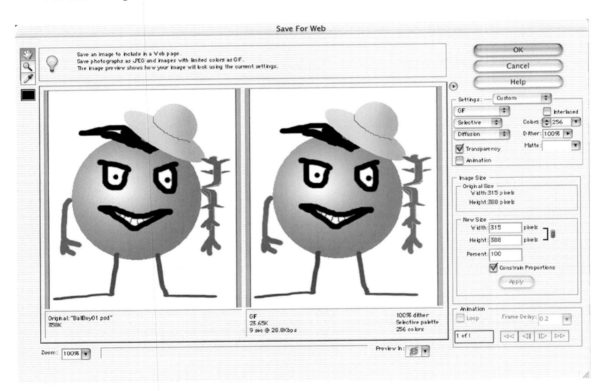

7. In the Settings pane at the top right of the window, select the GIF file format, don't worry too much about the other settings (unless you're a web expert and know what you want), and check the Animation button in the bottom left. Sadly the maximum number of colors in the GIF format is 256, so the quality might not always be great, but at least it can move. (Photoshop will reduce the colors to their nearest equivalents for you.) We'll see more about saving for the web in Chapter 7

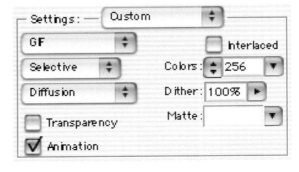

8. In the Animation pane we can choose how quickly our animation plays by setting the Frame Delay, measured in seconds. If we want our animation to cycle indefinitely we can check the Loop box. The DVD player style buttons can be used to check each frame sequentially.

9. Finally we click OK and save the image.

We now have a GIF file that can be put in any web page, as all major web browsers support the animated GIF format. OK, the animation here isn't great, and it was by no means easy to achieve (as you can only use one layer for each frame, so we lost the advantage of editing with layers) but a bit of motion can really bring a web site, or presentation, to life.

One way of using layers, and therefore animating like cell animators do, is to use one open Photoshop document with the layers in, move the layers as you see fit, then flatten it and copy the flattened layer to another document. Then return to the first document (on which you flattened the layers) and click Undo, which brings your uncompressed layer back. You can now make more changes, flatten, copy, and un-flatten until you've created as many frames as you want.

★ Three

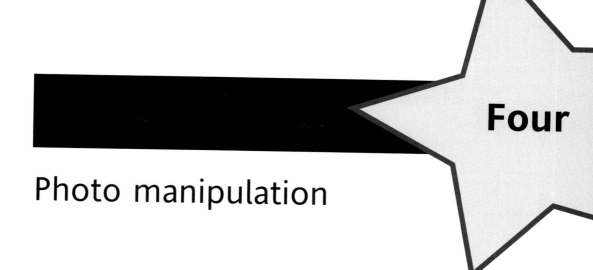

Four

Photo manipulation

In this chapter

If you've been working through the book in order, you must be itching to get your hands dirty by now. It's been a long time coming, but in this chapter we won't just be trimming the edges, or playing with layers, but actually using the tools with which Photoshop has built such an unrivaled reputation. In a few short pages, you too will have knowledge of the tricks of the magazine trade, including:

★ Using the Clone Stamp tool
★ Using the Dodge and Burn tools
★ Changing image texture
★ Using the Red Eye brush
★ Doctoring images
★ Looking younger
★ Making a panorama

Clone Stamp tool

We've seen a lot of clever features already in this book, and there are plenty more to come, but the ones that raise most interest are the ones that allow us to change people's appearance. A technique you'll commonly hear mentioned on TV is "airbrushing" (though in many places people now use the word "Photoshopped"). In Photoshop, the airbrush effect is done with the Clone Stamp tool. This is effectively a paintbrush that allows us to "paint" with patches of an image.

Spot removal

An obvious use of the Clone Stamp is to remove unsightly spots, or even perfectly natural aspects of appearance deemed unsuitable for viewing by advertising agencies and cosmetics vendors. Let's try that out on this lucky victim. This is example file Chapter04eg01.psd.

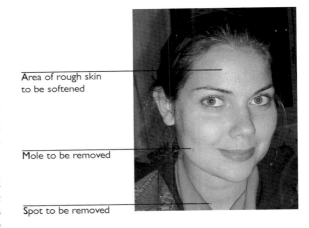

Area of rough skin to be softened

Mole to be removed

Spot to be removed

1. First we use the Zoom tool to close in on our first target imperfection – the mole. We don't need to go too close, or we won't be able to work, just near enough to have a clear view.

2. Next we need to select the Clone Stamp tool from the lower group of icons on the Toolbox. The following screenshot shows what the Options bar looks like when the Clone Stamp is selected.

Shows brush presets

Allows you to adjust size of brush withour resorting to presets

Select a blending mode for the brush (probably best to leave on Normal)

Copied point follows mouse at same distance

Adjust brushes opacity (flow strength)

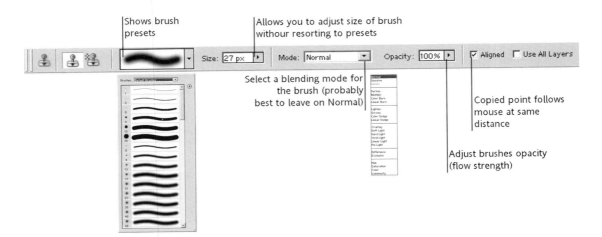

3. The next thing to do is to use the Options bar to select a suitably sized brush. This is the brush which we will be using to paint pixels from one area to another, and its size depends on how detailed we think the work will need to be.

In this example, we've gone for a soft-edged brush of 21 pixels as the brush head is about the same size as the mole. ('Soft-edged' refers to the feathering, or shading, around the brush so it is only 100% effective in the middle.)

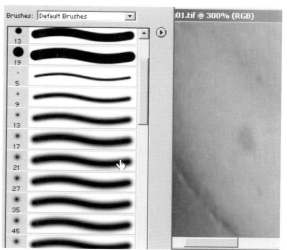

We can easily select the correct size brush by clicking on one of the previews, hovering the pointer over the image (where it will be represented by a circle showing its size) If it's the wrong size, simply select another one.

4. Ensure the Mode is set to Normal and, in this case as the area is an easy one, the Opacity is set to 100%.

5. To use the Clone Stamp, hold down the ALT key and click once near, but not on, your target (in this case the mole). While the ALT key is depressed, the mouse pointer will change into a crossed-hair style target.

The area we are selecting is the centre of the source for our cloning, though the size of the area cloned at any one time depends upon the brush we have chosen. We can repeat this step any time we like while using the Clone Stamp, just by pressing the ALT key and clicking somewhere else.

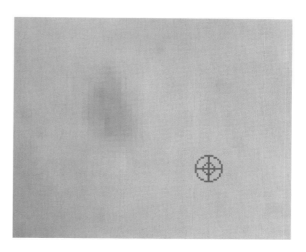

6. Having released the ALT key, we just move our mouse to the target area and stroke it across the offending object. It will copy the source area we selected over the area we are working on, and the source will move too – it will be kept equidistant from the first place you started painting. The behavior is similar to writing two letters at once by sticking two pens to either end of a ruler and writing with one of them.

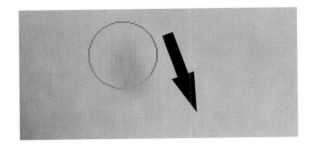

As we set the opacity high, it was quick and simple, but we didn't have a great deal of control over the final result. It's obviously an improvement, but at the same time there is a slight hint of it being too light now.

Delicate work

Patience is the watchword with most tasks using the Clone Stamp tool. Moles like the one we've seen already are easy to fix, because the surrounding area is of similar texture and color. Things get difficult when our flaw crosses different areas, as in this example image, where a hair has somehow got into our scanner.

If we're working along a lone line – like this hair – it's a good idea to keep sampling as often as possible. It is also worth ensuring that we follow the lines of the image if we've checked the handy Aligned checkbox on the Options bar. Follow the lines by ALT-clicking, then moving the mouse in the direction of the most obvious texture before you begin painting, as the arrows in the image do.

In this example image, we need to ALT+CLICK near the hair, with a small brush, then follow the lines of the image itself before painting with the selected area. We could also consider reducing the opacity and building up our image with clones from either side of our line. That way, if we go a little wrong, we won't ruin everything.

Use sample here

Another place to follow

Take sample here

Don't forget the handy Undo tool (CTRL/⌘+Z).

Dodging and burning

The Dodge and Burn tools are named after equivalent old photographic techniques for adding light to, or depriving light from, certain areas of an image. In Photoshop, they're another pair of brushes, similar to the Clone Stamp, which allow us to dodge (lighten) or burn (darken) patches of our image. The following image shows the Options bar when the Burn or Dodge tools are selected.

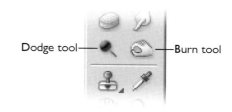

Dodge tool — Burn tool

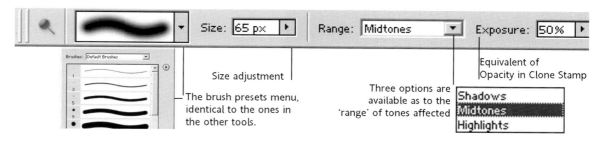

Size adjustment

The brush presets menu, identical to the ones in the other tools.

Three options are available as to the 'range' of tones affected

Equivalent of Opacity in Clone Stamp

Shadows
Midtones
Highlights

Dodge tool

The Dodge tool is especially useful for making changes to facial features, which can often have unwanted darker areas, especially in snaps that were only lit by a camera flash. In this image there are exaggerated dark areas under the eyes, but nothing too serious:

1. We start by selecting the Dodge tool.

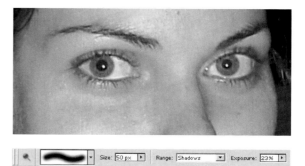

2. Then, we need to select Shadows from the Range drop-down menu on the Options bar (as we're only looking to lighten the dark areas), and a low Exposure setting (exposure is the equivalent of opacity – that is, how much effect the Dodge tool has). The size depends, as ever, on the image resolution.

3. Now, brush over the darker patches – we can go over and go over them to exaggerate the effect, but don't go too far. Remember that people looking at our picture shouldn't have their eyes immediately drawn to the patch we've edited – so a good tip is to keep zooming out to get an idea of the effect we are having on the image.

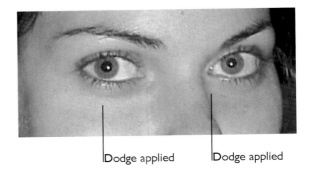

Dodge applied   Dodge applied

Burn tool

The Burn tool works in exactly the same way as the Dodge tool, but is well suited to a couple of surprising additions. It can do a great dark lipstick, and give quick and effective black eyes, (darkening skin-tones looks a lot like bruising) especially if we create a random mixture of larger and smaller brush sizes and play around with the Exposure setting. We can also use it to get a bit of "color" back into dodgy photocopies.

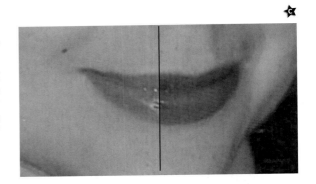

Texture changes

Quite apart from lightening and darkening patches of our image, there are a number of other 'point and play' tools we can use to fix trouble at the source. Sponge tool aside, these are all intuitively named, so you shouldn't have any trouble getting the hang of them.

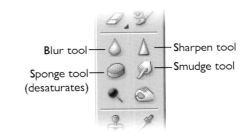

Blur tool — — Sharpen tool
Sponge tool — — Smudge tool
(desaturates)

Blur tool

The Blur tool works using the same brush engine ("engine" is programmer-slang for the code that drives a particular feature) as the Dodge and Burn tools above, though in action it can sometimes feel a little more sluggish as more computing work is needed. The larger the brush, the more you'll notice this. Here it has been used on the right hand side of the forehead to give a localized 'soft-focus' effect.

Sharpen tool

Blurring pixels is one thing, because it is a relatively straightforward process and we are, in effect, removing detail from the image. Adding detail is quite another matter, as, of course, there is no way for Photoshop to find information where there was none available to it in the first place. So sharpening is in fact a simulated effect, which exaggerates contrast between pixels.

The Sharpen tool also uses the brush engine described previously, and has been applied heavily in the left of this picture of a building site, and not at all on the right. It is pretty clear that the effect is initially to emphasize the edges of the pieces of rubble, but soon the effect becomes too strong, and just seems to be creating angular lumps of pixels.

Sponge tool

Not quite so obviously named as the others, the Sponge tool again harks back to an old technique. Here the Sponge is used to reduce, or (if Mode is set to Saturate) add color information to an image. In this example, the red flowers appeared too bright (right) so brushing the petals with a low-flowing (12%) Sponge reduced them a little, and so helped clarify the image.

Admittedly in this particular image, we might have done better to consider reducing the reds using one of the macro tools – the Hue/Saturation adjustment, for example – but in smaller areas a quick use of the Sponge tool is invaluable. Equally, exaggerating color in certain areas is just as quick and simple.

Smudge tool

The Smudge tool is another processor-intensive tool that can slow the computer down a little, but if we want the sort of artistic effect that it can achieve, it's worth persevering with. It is not the same as the Blur tool, which softens the appearance of the image by getting rid of detail. Instead it works by dragging the pixels we click on, and laying them behind in a line – about as close as a computer can get to smearing paint, especially

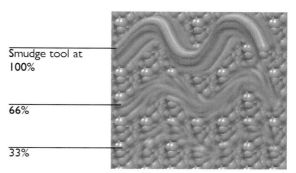

Smudge tool at 100%

66%

33%

if used with one of the more unusually shaped brushes further down the presets window.

It is difficult to suggest a specific photo-editing application for this tool, but it can be useful in creating effects, or can be combined with the artistic brushes (Chapter 6).

Red Eye Brush tool

Although your camera almost certainly has a feature designed to prevent it, many, many flash photos are marred by a phenomenon known as "red eye". Red eye is caused when the subject of the photo has dilated pupils, which cause the back of the eye to reflect light straight back at the camera. The darker the room before the flash was fired, the worse the effect is likely to be.

Although modern cameras have all got assorted methods of reducing this, they basically revolve around persuading the pupil to contract (a natural reaction to bright light), but typically end up causing the subject to close their eyes altogether! It would be far better to light the subject from further away from the lens (say with light reflected from the ceiling), but this is rarely possible. Instead, it's easier to do these things at the Photoshop stage, as we'll see now:

1. First, open the affected image and zoom into the eye area.

2. Then we select the Red Eye Brush tool.

   A rather daunting Options bar appears, and at this point it helps to think of the tool not just for replacing rogue reds, but also as a more versatile color replacement tool. After all, Photoshop can't tell an eye from any other collection of pixels, but it does know what color they all are.

3. By default Sampling should be set to First Click. If not, we need to change it. This means that, wherever we first click with the brush, until you release it, the color underneath will be the target color to replace.

4. For this example, we need to select a small brush; a simple round one will be sufficient.

5. Then we point the brush over the red area of the eye – the color under the crossed-hairs will be reflected in the Current color box on the Options bar. We just click to begin the stroke of the brush that will recolor our eye – the default is black, which is usually appropriate (remember, this is the pupil, not the colored area of the eye). The replacement color will be a shade of the selected color, the stronger the color being replaced, the darker the shade of the replacement used.

   We can select another replacement color by clicking on the Replacement color box on the Options bar.

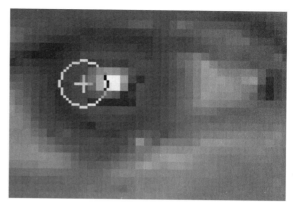

6. Now we just need to repeat these steps for the other eye – it doesn't mater if the red is different in the next eye as Photoshop re-samples the color to be replaced each time you click.

> *The Tolerance works in exactly the same way as on the Magic Wand tool – if you are replacing too many, or too few, colors, adjust it.*

Doctoring images

We can remove red eye with a lot of different software packages these days, some of which are given away free with cameras, or scanners, but if you've added Photoshop to your armory, you're probably a little more ambitious than that. By combining the subtlety of the image-editing tools with the power of the layers we can make much more significant changes to our photos, though obviously we need to start being more careful about realism.

New skies

It's always the same, isn't it? You travel hundreds, or even thousands of miles to see a tourist attraction (admittedly, Symphony Hall, Birmingham UK only loosely counts!) only to find that the weather spoils it for you. Well, no problem at all – we can easily spruce up a photo like this by applying a new sky.

1. We start by opening up the weather-spoiled image and duplicating the background layer (by dragging the Background layer to the New Layer icon at the bottom left of the Layers palette).

2. Next, we turn off the visibility of the lower (Background) layer. Hopefully, we won't need it again, but it's worth having it just in case.

3. Now we select the sky area – if it is a dull, monotonous grey like this one, the Magic Wand should be ideal.

4. Next we feather our selection by a small amount – 2 pixels should be enough for this image (which is at 300dpi), any more and we'll end up with a halo effect on our final object.

5. Now hit the DELETE key (or click Edit > Cut), and deselect (Ctrl/⌘+D) the area.

   At this stage, we should be left with our original image, minus its sky, on a fully editable layer. We now have two choices, we could either find a sky and lay our image on top of it, or tuck a sky in behind it. We'll go for the latter, as it's easier to scale a sky (they have less detail and are usually only focused at infinity, rather than the crisp focus on nearer objects).

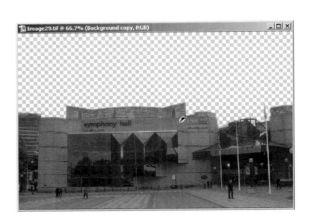

6. Leaving our edited target image open (though for peace of mind, this is a good point at which to save at), we open our sky image (Chapter04eg03sky.psd) and make it the active image.

7. Now we need to drag the layer that our sky's on (in this case, the Background layer of the sky image) from the Layers palette and drop it anywhere in the image where the new sky is needed. It then appears at the top of the Layers palette for that original image. Any layer can be copied into another image in this way.

8. Next, we need to click on the newly copied layer, and select the Move tool. Corner handles will appear which we can use to expand it to at least the width of the original image (remember to hold down SHIFT to preserve the proportions of the layer)

9. Next we need to move the sky layer below our target image layer. In this example image, we can still use the Move tool to move the sky a bit as there is more blue sky hidden beneath the building.

★ **Four**

10. Once we're happy with the position of our sky, the final step is to compensate for the change in apparent lighting conditions. To do this, we click on the Background Copy layer (or any more sensible name that you used) and then click Layers > New Adjustment Layer > Levels…

11. In the New Layer dialog we need to check the Group With Previous Layer box (that's why we used the menu command in step 10 rather than the handy button at the bottom of the palette, because it opens this dialog).

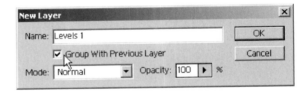

12. We now make whatever levels adjustments we feel are necessary – they're previewed on screen as we adjust the sliders.

If we're using a sky with an obviously different hue, we could consider applying a Solid Color adjustment layer at a low opacity, or a Hue/Saturation adjustment.

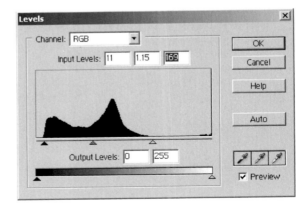

13. When we're happy, we can flatten the layers by selecting Flatten Image from the Layers palette More menu This does lose the insurance layer though!

The final image is by no means perfect – these things rarely are – but it certainly looks like a nicer day now. Judicious use of the Dodge and Burn tools could make some areas (like the office tower being built on the left) blend in better.

Remember though, you'll never be convinced by your own work because you *know* what you did, the aim is to fool others.

Family photo

A similar approach is possible with group photographs too, though it might involve a little more work with the layers. In this example, mum wasn't available one of the wedding day photos, but we're going to have to put her back in. For your own shots, identify a group shot and someone else to add to that group from another photo. Here we're going to make life as difficult for ourselves as possible by selecting someone who is partially obscured, from an image taken under different lighting. Clearly it's sensible not to make extra work for yourself unless you have to!

1. Start by opening your background image, and make any adjustments to the levels and lighting you think fit. It is important to get this out of the way, as we will be working with partial duplicates of the same layer.

2. Then select the image of the transplant victim, and open it alongside the target image in Photoshop. In our example, the victim is the woman behind the flowers, the groom's mum. You may find that this slows your machine down a little.

3. The next task is to select her as accurately as possible – mistakes are more obvious with people than with other objects. We'll start with the Lasso tool, selecting loosely around the target, and then tidy up the selection using other tools, like the Magic Wand.

4. You'll need to use whatever techniques are necessary to select the victim. Here we're also going to include the flowers for the time being. Be very careful when checking the selection – notice how the Magic Wand has removed the handbag shoulder strap in the comparison image here. That needs to be added back in.

5. If the original is on a noticeably different colored background, it's a good idea to bring the selection in just a little, by clicking Select > Modify > Contract... as it's better to very slightly trim your victim than give them a halo of the other background color.

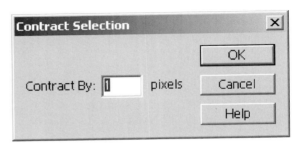

6. Next, we need to Feather our selection (Select > Feather...) with a low value, although depending on the resolution. Here we've used 2 pixels, which fits nicely with the slight soft-focus feel of the original.

7. Now, with both images open, and the source image the "live" window, we select the Move tool and drag the victim across to the other window.

   There's no need to worry about any mess we make of the original – there's no need to save it. We can now close that window.

8. With the selection in the new image, we can press CTRL/⌘+T to select the Free Transform tool, which we can use to scale the woman to the right size.

Remember to hold SHIFT to maintain the correct proportions.

9. Also using the Move tool, we can drag her to the correct position on the page. It's here where we start to see how much of a problem the flowers are going to be. The solution is to move her behind the people, but not the background.

10. To do this, we make the new layer (Victim) invisible, and select the original (Original Group) layer to work on.

11. Then using the selection tools, we need to select and highlight the group, as we did with the woman before, paying particular attention to the left-hand end, where it will have to overlap with our new "guest".

12. After we've made the selection, we should apply a single pixel feather so the edges aren't too sharp – CTRL/⌘+ALT+D brings up the feathering dialog.

13. Next, we select Layer > New Layer by Copy, which will create a new layer containing just our selected people. We need to drag this to the top of the Layers palette, and then make the new person layer visible again.

That should be our basic result achieved. Now all we need to do is compensate for the problems in the original source image, like the flowers, and any levels issues.

14. Now we're going to need to work on making a few changes to the woman we've added. We can use Photoshop's layers to help us out, by reducing the opacity of the top layer, then selecting the layer beneath it to work on. This way, we can see where we need to work with the Clone Stamp.

15. Selecting the Clone Stamp tool from the toolbox and ensuring that the Use All Layers option at the far right of the Options bar is *not* selected, we can begin hiding the areas of flowers that aren't hidden by the ghost. With a complicated pattern like this, we can often get better results with a hard edged brush, as softer ones can create blurring.

16. We also need to reduce the effect of the camera flash on the glasses (there wouldn't have been a flash outside). This is also done with the Clone Stamp but a much smaller brush, with soft edges and a lower opacity.

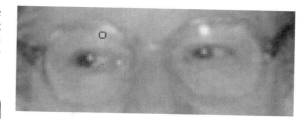

If we were feeling really ambitious, we might try and move the eyes a little, so that they appear to be looking at the camera. We could do this by:

★ Selecting both eyes (a single click with a soft edged Selection Brush tool seems appropriate here, given the low resolution).
★ Creating another new layer via copying, and making it temporarily invisible.
★ Removing the pupils of the eyes on the original layer with the Clone Stamp tool.
★ Making the eye pupil layer visible, then nudging it a couple of pixels over into place using the arrow keys.
★ Using the Dodge/Burn tools to tidy this up and to minimize camera flash.

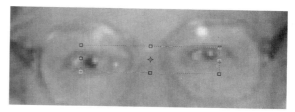

17. At this point, depending on the conditions the images were taken in, you may want to apply some adjustment layers to the added character (and, possibly, their eyes) to make it fit in with the rest of the image, as in steps 10-12 of the Symphony Hall image. In this example we're also going to add a slight blur to her layer, by selecting Filter > Blur > Gaussian Blur (at 0.5 pixels) to compensate for the main image's less sharp focus.

18. Finally, we can use the Dodge and Burn tools, on low strengths, to apply shadow onto anyone now tucked in behind someone else.

The final result: all the family together in one scene! Of course, there are plenty of other uses for the same techniques, for example adding yourself to your favorite football team's line-up photo (well, it takes less time than all the practice and waiting to be spotted by a scout). You could also try just using a head and pasting it onto someone else's neck, if you felt that way inclined...

Taking years off

One of the first things you hear about image editors is their ability to make people look younger. True, of course, but the watchword here is subtlety. The further you get from the original image, the less the chance of anyone mistaking it for someone just looking a little fresher the day the portrait was taken. Basically, we live in a world where most people are technology-savvy, and if something doesn't look completely convincing, they'll doubt it.

With those thoughts in mind, we'll take this picture of a distinguished old gent, and see if we can't make him look a little younger.

1. We'll begin by opening up the image and performing a simple levels adjustment (see Chapter 3 if you're unsure how).

2. Now we duplicate the background layer by dragging it onto the New Layer icon at the bottom right of the Layers palette. The copied layer is especially handy when doing age-reduction, and indeed any work on people as we can quickly turn on and off the visibility of the foreground layer to judge if what we are doing still looks believable.

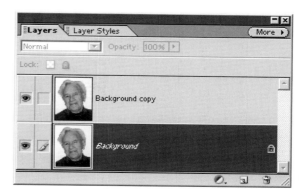

3. Some would say that we need to identify all the areas that we're going to target (as shown in the following image), but we find that approach is a bit too constricting. We prefer to target areas as we go along, as there is tendency not to see everything at first. Some things become more obvious as we get rid of others. It is up to you though.

Hair lighter than eyebrows (quite a big change to make, will be noticed)

Marks on the skin need to be softened

Area under eyes shows age, especially in 40s and up.

Wrinkles are the most obvious thing to see and remove (and where we will start with this picture)

Whiter teeth and more pronounced lips will help

4. The best place to start is the wrinkles, which should be attacked with the Clone Stamp. What we'll do is remove the smaller ones completely, then look at toning down some of the others with a lower opacity brush. First we'll zoom into the target zone, but not so close that we lose sense of what we're doing, and then select a soft-edged brush. We just select 100% opacity and simply copy from alongside the wrinkle. With a bit of practice, it can be done in one swift stroke.

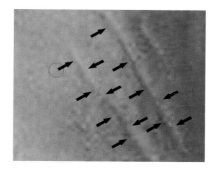

Something to watch out for is "banding" – this means a result like that in the image on the right where, because of not taking new samples and working too closely, the same data has been copied across the image. This is usually fixed by making sure we are using the right sized brush head and taking new ALT samples occasionally, possibly from different sides.

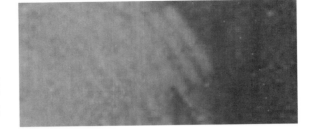

5. We continue like this and tackle all of the smaller wrinkles in the image. A good tip is to look for ones in similar places on the opposite side of the face. The following image shows the wrinkles before and after our treatment.

6. To make more subtle changes to the deeper wrinkles, we need to set our Clone Stamp to a lower opacity – about 30% – and then just lightly apply surrounding tones to the deeper wrinkles. We don't want to remove them completely. (Always select the cloned pixels from the lighted slide of the wrinkle). Don't forget the neck at this second stage!

Before we do that, now might also be a good chance to take a copy layer at this stage and call it 1st Wrinkles or something similar, just in case.

7. We can use much the same lightening technique, as we used for the deeper wrinkles, on the blotchy areas on either side of the forehead. The has the double advantage of diminishing the texture a little because of the softness of our brush.

8. Finally with the Clone Stamp, we can remove the spot in the middle tip of the nose, and the blemish on (his) right cheek. The before and after progress from the last image looks like this:

9. The next step is a bit of dentistry. For this example we've used the Dodge tool (for lightening areas), with a 50% exposure, small, hard-edged brush. We've brushed over the teeth to lighten them a little – we don't want to do it too much or it'll look like he is in an American soap opera! We can also apply this technique to the whites of the eyes.

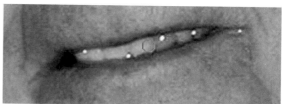

10. The next thing to do is select the Burn tool, with a very low exposure (15%), and go over the bottom and top lips slightly to darken them. Following that, we can use the Sponge tool, on an equally low Flow level. In both cases, we've taken care not to go outside the lip area.

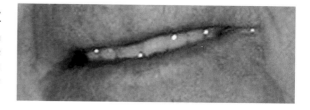

11. Now, we need to take a new copy of our layer, and zoom out so we can see the whole face. In this example, we've called the new layer Soft.

12. Using the Magic Wand tool we can select an area of the forehead by clicking in it. If we continue to add to this selection by SHIFT+clicking in areas of the face which are smooth – cheeks, etc, the result should be that we're left with all of the lower detail areas of the face highlighted.

13. We can now inverse the selection by pressing CTRL/⌘+SHIFT+I or by clicking Select > Inverse, so that now all the detailed areas of the face are highlighted.

If necessary, we can still add some of the "complicated" areas of the face (eyes, wrinkles, ears, etc) to the highlighted area by holding SHIFT and Lassoing manually.

14. This selection needs feathering by about 4 pixels (more for a higher resolution image).

15. The next thing to do is to delete the selected complicated areas from the layer, by clicking Edit > Cut or pressing CTRL/⌘+X so we are effectively left with a mask (in the non-technical sense of the word!) as your top layer. If you're of a nervous disposition you could also take a copy of this, turn off its visibility and lock it.

16. Now we make all our layers visible again, and select the top layer (the spooky mask we just created).

17. If we then click Filter > Blur > Gaussian Blur, we have an adjustable "mask", which can be blurred by adjusting the slider. This way, we can apply an even blur, and judge how far to go (before clicking OK). It is personal choice at which point the skin stops looking younger and starts looking plastic – we think 1.0 on this particular image.

An alternative to steps 11-17 would be to use the Blur tool on a low opacity, but by comparison it is harder to get it even. In addition, we can't turn off the Blur tool later if we decide we don't like it.

18. Finally, though it's probably only worth trying in the most extreme of circumstances, we can apply the Burn brush to the hair for a reasonably convincing darkening effect, depending on the type. In this case it might be seen as a step too far, but we've definitely lost ten years before this.

That's about it really. In our final image, we've taken out a large number of wrinkles, but left some, albeit lighter than they were, so that our work isn't completely unconvincing. We've also given him a quick tooth brushing, and smoothed areas of the skin a bit to give a younger looking texture. Finally, we've capped it all off with the slightly extravagant touch of darkening the hair, though perhaps it was a step too far!

Photomerge

Sometimes a single frame doesn't do a view justice, and the only solution is to take a series of images of our location and stick them together in a row. Many an old fashioned photo-album has images stuck together with tape, or held next to each other one way or another. Now, predictably, we can do this in Photoshop too. Here we have open 4 shots taken, from left to right, of a regeneration project in Birmingham, UK. Admittedly it isn't the best of views, but it features some complicated shapes and will be difficult to line up at the best of times. Not only that but, contrary to all advice, they were taken by hand, without a tripod.

1. Click File > Create Photomerge… and a dialog will come up featuring all the images currently open in Photoshop. If your images are listed, as these are, just click OK. If there are any you don't want, click once on their name then click remove. Alternatively you can browse the computer as you would to open a file.

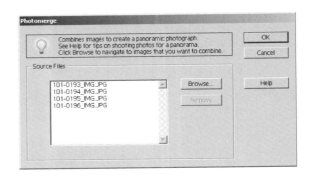

2. The computer will now attempt to join all the images, and open up a window featuring a rough panorama.

You may get this warning. Don't worry, all is not lost. You will have the chance of trying again to persuade Photoshop where to put it.

3. We are now taken to a dialog box outside Photoshop with unfamiliar tools to the left and some options to the right:

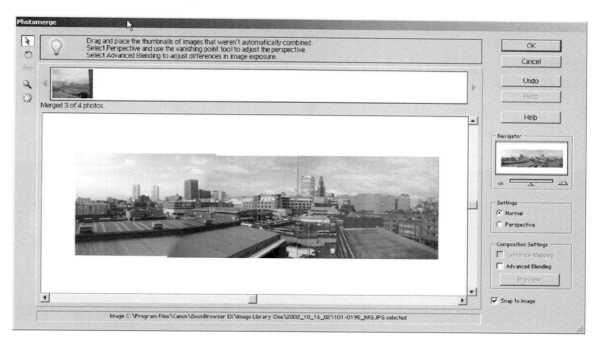

Our first task from this window is to arrange all the thumbnails (from the top bar) in order in the main panorama. Simply drag each (or the remaining) thumbnail towards its position in the main image.

4. While your dragging an image, it becomes slightly transparent so you can line it up the best you can to the rest of the panorama. Do this, then let go of the mouse button and Photoshop will have a go at lining them up.

At this point we could simply click OK and be left with a pretty complete montage – certainly a better result than before we started. But we can take it a little further too, depending on the number of images we are using.

Look closely at the truck in this compilation, or the rightmost join. They don't quite line up, do they? What is needed is a perspective correction, which is our next step.

5. Click on the Perspective option in the Settings box. This will try and compensate for the perspective of your photos by scaling images around the **Vanishing Point** into trapezoids so that they fit more comfortably. The vanishing point image is assumed to be the middle one (though you can change this with the Set Vanishing Point tool   ).

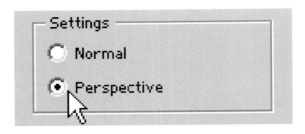

Again this may produce an error message, if the perspective is especially strong. In which case we'll be left – as we are in the next image – with one of the images left unaltered, and ruining our perspective effect.

We can try dragging it there ourselves, but it might be beyond Photomerge to stretch it. In this case we'll see this error message and, to be honest, if we want the perspective effect it isn't worth fighting it.

6. For this example, we'll just put the unwanted image in the thumbnail bar at the top and carry on with the three images (Photomerge seems happier with an odd number anyway).

This is another stage at which we could click OK and Photomerge will get on with the process of producing our final merge as a new file in Photoshop (though we may well need to crop a lot of the wider perspective parts.

7. Alternatively we can try out a couple of extra features available to smooth things out a bit:

★ **Cylindrical Mapping** is a way of making perspectivized images fit each other without the bow-tie effect.
★ **Advanced Blending** which attempts to smooth out contrast differences between your images – definitely necessary here!

Click preview.

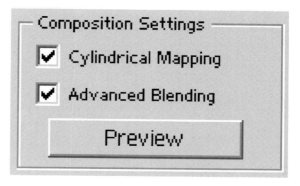

8. The preview results are very encouraging, all that we need to do now is to click OK and wait.

Not really much better, is it? The join on the right is pretty faultless except some contrast in the sky. The other, however, is much less convincing. Before we do anything with this, we might want to tidy this up a little. Our tactic will be to apply an adjustment layer to the area to the right of the image.

9. Select the area that seems obviously wrong using the Polygonal Lasso tool and a feather of around 10 pixels (to match the fade that Photomerge has applied).

10. Now create a Levels adjustment layer (or any kind that seems appropriate to you). The layer will automatically be masked so that only the area you highlighted is affected by your changes. You'll need to make whatever changes seem appropriate to your image.

11. You may need to further alter the mask – in this layer, for example, Photomerge has done a good job of smoothing the skies, but less so the roof areas. My tactic is to draw a gradient in the selected area of the adjustment layer, so the sky is masked out on the adjustment layer. (For more on masking, see Chapter 3).

> You are essentially compensating for your camera's auto modes here. If you take all the images with the same shutter speed etc. then they should (in theory) all work well together, though some areas of the panorama might then be bleached or dark depending on the lighting.

12. Once you're happy with making overall changes using masked adjustment layers, flatten the image.

13. Another tactic is to use a soft-edged Clone Stamp tool to get rid of the harsh lines, especially in areas where it doesn't matter too much about detail, like the sky. This is much harder if you haven't flattened your image.

In this image, where the left join crossed some buildings, it was possible to use the Clone Stamp tool to extend horizontal/vertical edges on the buildings that the line crossed diagonally. You will have to choose your tactics depending on your image.

14. Finally, crop your image to the final size, getting rid of any white areas.

Still by no means perfect, but at least the most jarring edges have been removed. Welcome to Birmingham UK – not, admittedly, the most attractive image to make a panorama of, but the edges showed what Photoshop's Photomerge tool is, and is not, capable of.

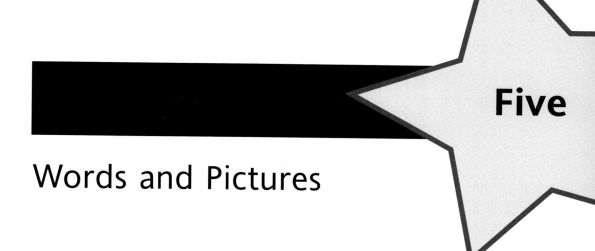

Words and Pictures

In this chapter

In this chapter, we look at some of the things that Photoshop has made its own. Text used to be the preserve of word processors, or dedicated page layout packages, geometrical shapes used to be the preserve of expensive illustration applications. However, by using very similar techniques (because the computer thinks of text and shapes in very similar ways), we can now do all this without leaving Photoshop (and make it look better, too). In this chapter we're going to look at:

★ Adding text
★ Importing text from a word processor
★ Making text bend
★ Adding styles to text
★ Adding text to images
★ Creating text from images
★ Shapes
★ The Shape tools
★ Making your own shapes

How text is displayed

Traditionally, in so far as the computer industry is old enough to have traditions, text and geometric shapes have been regarded as the preserve of vector graphics programs, like Adobe Illustrator. That is because it is much easier for a computer to describe a shape in terms of its lines and angles, and makes it possible to scale graphics indefinitely. That is why all the fonts on our systems are constructed in this way, so we can make them any size we want, and all the computer has to do is follow the instructions to draw them, smoothly, at any size.

If we're going to produce complicated schematics, then dedicated vector graphics programs are probably still the best way to go, but if we want to put words with our pictures, or use simple shapes for web graphics (which have to be bitmaps in the end) then we can now achieve this in Photoshop without losing much of the flexibility or scalability associated with vectors.

It works a little like this: when we are working with the text or graphics layer, it behaves like a vector layer, we can scale it, edit it, and distort it with the same flexibilty and without ever developing the jagged edges that zooming a pixel graphic would have. But when we flatten it, print it, or export, it Photoshop looks where those lines should be on the page, and draws a layer with pixels following the imaginery lines.

The shaded pixels in the example are due to an effect called anti-aliasing, which uses a shade of the text color (depending on how much of the shape would be inside that pixel) to "smooth out" the image (we can turn this effect off if we want).

These resizing calculations are handled automatically by Photoshop each time we print/export. So, as long as the text or shape layer remains a text or shape layer (that is we keep our work in Photoshop PSD format), we can still change the shapes. Here, for example, we've vertically stretched the letters by 50%. The lines have been redrawn (the pixels underneath are not stretched) and the anti-aliasing has been redrawn to take into account the new position of the vector shapes.

The same principles apply to shapes drawn using the Shape tools.

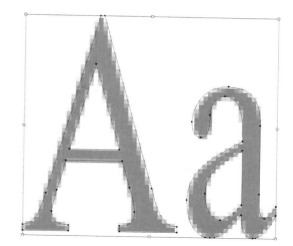

Adding text

To understand this section, as you may have gathered from the above, requires a bit of an understanding of layers, but we'll try not to get as in-depth as Chapter 3 (which is where you'll find out everything else about layers, should you need it). That's principally because the Type tool adds a new layer for each new piece of Text we add.

The best way to get the hang of the basics is to add something to our document, so let's get going.

1. We'll start by selecting the Type tool. The following image shows both of the two tool Options bars that we'll see.

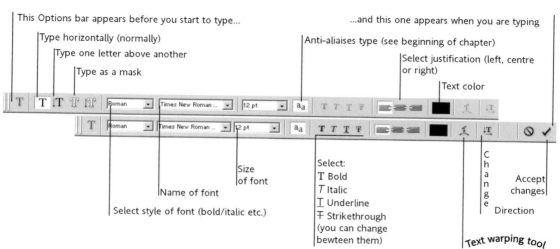

This Options bar appears before you start to type...

Type horizontally (normally)

Type one letter above another

Type as a mask

...and this one appears when you are typing

Anti-aliaises type (see beginning of chapter)

Select justification (left, centre or right)

Text color

Size of font

Name of font

Select style of font (bold/italic etc.)

Select:
T Bold
T Italic
T̲ Underline
T̶ Strikethrough
(you can change bewteen them)

Change Direction

Accept changes

Text warping tool

129

Having the two Options bars can seem a needlessly complicated approach, but in reality Photoshop is merely depriving us of a few tools that we can't use anyway.

Also, there are two places to select "bold" or "italic" typefaces, which might seem equally confusing, but in reality the dropdown on the far left is selecting from subsets of the font, and the buttons on the right just stretch or slant the letters a bit. It is always preferable to use the font subsets if possible, the faux fonts are a last resort.

2. The next thing to do is to select the Horizontal Type tool (the default), then click somewhere in the image window and we can begin typing whatever we like.

3. If we want to make changes to our text, we just need to highlight it, as in a word-processor, by clicking at one point of the required text and dragging to another point.

4. We can then use any part of the Type tool's Options bar to change our text – the typeface, bold/italic etc, or even the color. The changes are only applied to the highlighted text. In this case we'll change to Bold font subset.

Alternatively, if we change our mind about writing horizontally (and discarded millennia of western thought at the same time) we can click on the Change Text Orientation button at the far right of the Options bar. This button, unlike the font and color options, affects all the text currently being edited.

Notice how the Type layer appears in the Layers palette – instead of a thumbnail of the contents with a lot of transparency, all we get is a "T". This means that the text layer is still editable, and the areas that don't have text in are always transparent. The layer is also named automatically, using the first 30 letters of the text we added.

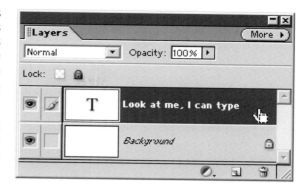

To edit the text later, we just select the Type tool from the toolbox then click somewhere over the words we want to edit, and the layer will be automatically selected.

Using text from a word processor

So, in summary, the text editor is easy. But it's probably still pretty basic compared to your word processor of choice. Let's face it, lacking in graphical capabilities though it might be, Microsoft Word (or Works) is still pretty handy when it comes to writing; it can check spelling, for one thing. That's why Photoshop can also import your words from a word processor. Let's try this out:

1. We simply highlight and copy some words (not too many at once is advisable) using our word-processor's "Copy" function (almost universally CTRL/⌘+C).

2. Then we click where we want our text to start in the image window, and then select a font size and style.

3. Finally, we paste the text from the clipboard by pressing CTRL/⌘+V (again this should be familiar from your word processor).

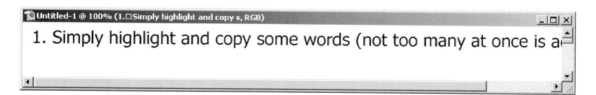

You can instantly see the problem with this technique; the text all appears in one line (despite the fact that in Word it was automatically broken up to fit within its margins), and all the formatting has been lost.

The alternative is to copy the text as before, but not to use the Type tool at all. Simply select the background layer in the Layers palette, and then paste directly into the Photoshop window. Photoshop will create a new layer with the text rasterized on it. This time we have retained the formatting from Word, including the new lines. However, we've lost our control on the text in Photoshop.

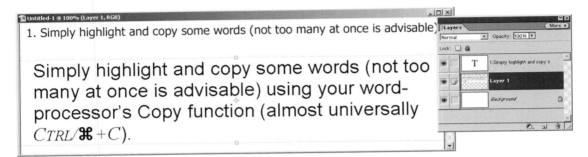

This is because the text has been simplified (rasterized) into pixels as part of the conversion process, and given the same white background it had in Word, so it's now an image rather than normal text. We can do the same thing to our Type layers by selecting them in the Layers palette and then choosing Simplify Layer from the More menu. Unless we're planning on applying an effect we can't achieve without pixels, though, it's a bad move, as we lose all the advantages of vector graphics described above.

Shaping text

A nice effect to make our writing a little bit more fun, or to help it fit into the style of an image, is to bend it around a bit. Photoshop's Type comes with a very comprehensive set of preset bends, which we can adjust to suit our own needs. Let's see how they work:

1. First, we need to type in some text with the Type tool, as above. For this example we'll use SHAPETASTIC.

2. Then click on the Warp button (towards the right-hand end of the Options bar).

3. We can now choose a shape from the Style dropdown. The little shapes show the "envelope" that our words will be fitted into (all still done using vectors). The following image shows the effect the Fish style has on our text:

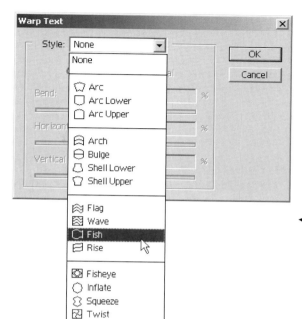

SHAPETASTIC

4. The Bend, Horizontal, and Vertical Distortion sliders now become available, which we can use to modify our chosen style.

Adjusting the Bend will increase or decrease the effect of the distortion, and the results will be previewed on-screen as we work. Here it has been increased so far that part of the envelope has criss-crossed, leading to an upside-down letter effect.

With the bend set to 0, a positive horizontal distortion always makes the later letters larger.

A negative horizontal distortion has the opposite effect:

Positive vertical distortion.

Negative vertical distortion.

5. We can adjust the sliders until we're happy with our shape, and then click OK. This arrangement, for example, has this result:

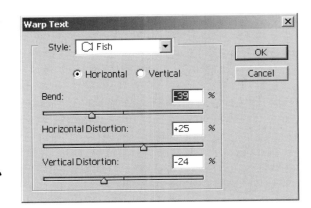

The fantastic thing is that, when we click OK, our layer is still a fully editable type layer, not a simplified pixel layer. That means we can still edit the text, or transform it, without losing any of the benefits of vectors explained above. For example, we can insert a dash, without losing the style we just chose.

The following is a quick rundown of all the styles. Unless otherwise mentioned, they are styled with a 25% bend, and no horizontal or vertical change. The first few are shown in both positive and negative to give an idea of the effect it has.

Arc (positive bend):

SHAPE-TASTIC

Arc (negative bend):

SHAPE-TASTIC

Arc Lower (positive):

SHAPE-TASTIC

Arc Lower (negative bend):

SHAPE-TASTIC

Arc Upper (positive bend):

SHAPE-TASTIC

Arc Upper (negative bend):

SHAPE-TASTIC

Arch (positive bend):

SHAPE-TASTIC

Bulge (positive bend):

SHAPE-TASTIC

Shell Lower:

SHAPE-TASTIC

Shell Upper:

SHAPE-TASTIC

Flag:

SHAPE-TASTIC

Wave (at +50%):

SHAPE-TASTIC

Fish:

SHAPE-TASTIC

Rise:

SHAPE-TASTIC

Fish Eye:

SHAPE-TASTIC

Inflate:

SHAPE-TASTIC

Squeeze:

SHAPE-TASTIC

Twist:

SHAPE-TASTIC

We can apply the styles in a horizontal manner, as we have above, or vertically, by clicking on the Vertical button. This doesn't work with Fish Eye, Inflate, or Twist, as they already affect the text in both directions. It can also lead to slightly disappointing results because it works on the whole space the computer leaves for the characters, whether they are there or not. For example, there is a lot of space for lowercase letters with tails, which Photoshop doesn't take into account when producing only capitals – as can be seen in the cursor here.

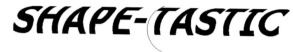

Word and pictures

Another thing we can do to text layers is apply layer styles to them, giving the letters a little bit more character, as it were, and (more practically) helping them stand out against photographic backgrounds, which are often quite complicated. Let's say we want to add the text "Bus Route 50: Bradford Street" to our image:

1. Open an image you want to add text to, or use the example (Chapter05eg01.jpg).

2. First, we select the Type tool and add our text, using any style, and any warping that we choose. Here we've using 18pt Tahoma Bold.

3. Next, we click the Options bar tick to accept the text.

4. Making sure that our text layer is the active (highlighted) layer in the Layers palette, open the Layer Styles palette.

5. We can of course choose anything we like here, but a good choice when making black text stand out is to apply an outer glow (a shadow has a similar effect on white text). To apply it, we need to select Outer Glows from the drop-down menu at the top of the box, and then click on the Simple layer.

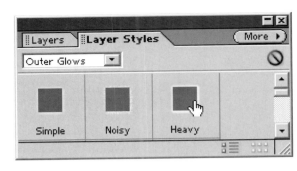

6. If the text is small, we might need to alter the glow's settings. We can do this by returning to the Layers palette and double-clicking on the "F" icon that appears to the right of the Text layer.

7. This brings up the Style Settings dialog, which allows us to adjust the size of the glow. A close glow is ideal for the text as it acts much like an outline.

The next two images show our final result on the left, and what we would have got if we'd been more adventurous with our styles (and selected Groovy from the Complex list) on the right:

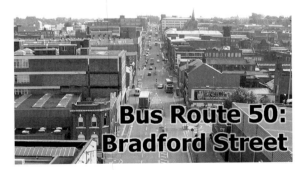
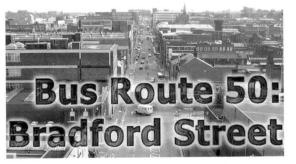

When experimenting with layer styles, remember to use the button at the top right-hand corner to remove them, otherwise they will be applied on top of each other, which can get quite confusing, not to mention slowing down the computer. The upside of this is that we can combine styles; an inner glow, and a shadow, for example, to create our own effects.

Words from pictures

Taking a picture and turning it into a word is always a popular effect, and the Type Masking tools make it easier to achieve than ever. Once you've completed it, you can incorporate it into other images easily thanks to Layers. Let's have a go:

1. Open an image that you want to use as your background image. We'll use the skyline created in Chapter 4.

2. We need to select the Horizontal Mask Type tool (from the Type tool) and choose a typeface and size. If we're just doing one word, the center justify is a sensible choice too.

3. Now we click where we wish to begin typing from and type in our word.

4. We need to be sure we're happy before clicking the tick to accept changes, as unlike regular text, we can't go back.

5. We now have our future word selected, and a number of options open to us. We can either:

- ★ Inverse the selection (CTRL/⌘+I) then delete the remaining portion of the image, leaving the word on the one layer.

- ★ Create a version of the word on its own layer so effects can more easily be applied to it. This is done by selecting Layer > New > Layer via Copy, and is what we'll do. This will, temporarily, make our text disappear.

6. We can now add layer effects to our words (or drag the layer to another image altogether). We'll go for the former here by switching to the Layer Styles palette. Here, adding a Low drop shadow gives an interesting effect. We could leave it here...

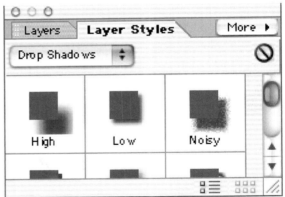

7. ...or obliterate the layer below so we can see what's going on more clearly.

Shapes

As well as allowing us to use vector graphics to create text in a huge variety of different styles, Photoshop Elements allows us to create scaleable shape layers. In reality, these tools are really a simplified version of the drawing tools you would get in a fully-fledged vector graphics program, like Adobe Illustrator and when using them it's important not to get over ambitious. We can create shapes, or use some of the catalogue of pre-defined ones, to help illustrate our images or make web graphics, but not much more than that. However, what Photoshop lacks here, it more than makes up for by allowing us to combine layers styles with these shapes to create interesting, varied and high-quality output. In fact, a lot of the illustrations in this book were actually prepared using Elements (yes, the ones with the single lines in – alright, not as clever as all that, we admit.)

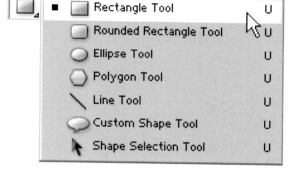

Using the shape tools

At first, the shape tools might not seem immediately intuitive, especially if you have used other vector programs. The most perplexing aspect is thinking in shape layers, which have been designed to fit in seamlessly with the rest of the layers we've already looked at. Any one layer can contain as many individual shapes as we like, overlapping or not, and will be considered one shape by Photoshop. All shapes on that layer have to be the same color, and will act in unison during operations like applying of styles, or moving. Within that layer, we can move and adjust shapes using the Shape Selection tool, but not change their color. The following image shows the shape tools' Options Bar:

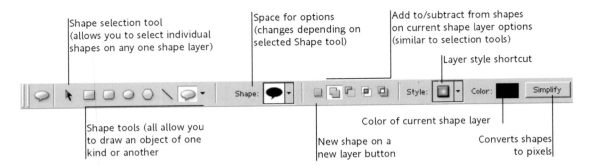

Shape selection tool
(allows you to select individual
shapes on any one shape layer)

Space for options
(changes depending on
selected Shape tool)

Add to/subtract from shapes
on current shape layer options
(similar to selection tools)

Layer style shortcut

Shape tools (all allow you
to draw an object of one
kind or another)

New shape on a
new layer button

Color of current shape layer

Converts shapes
to pixels

Lets not get carried away though, a lot of the time we are only going to want to use one of the pre-defined shapes. Drawing a shape is a lot like using the Marquee tools, or the Free Transform tool:

1. Start a new Photoshop document (we can, of course, put things on top of pictures, but for our purposes it would look a little cluttered).

2. Select the Custom Shape tool from the Options Bar.

3. Now we can choose a shape we like by clicking on the drop-down arrow and having a look at the built-in shapes. The speech bubble can be very effective in altering the meanings of our photos, but for now we'll settle on the lovely heart. We need to double click on it's thumbnail to select it.

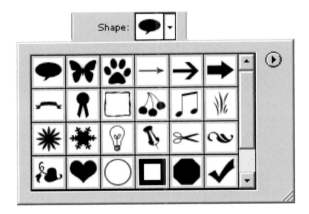

4. To position the shape, we need to click in the top left of where we want it to be and drag the mouse to the bottom right. We can hold down SHIFT to maintain the original proportions.

That's all there is to it. We can change the color at any time if you're still using any of the shape tools (except the Shape Selection tool) and clicking in the color box on the Options bar.

5. We can modify our heart to look a lot nicer if we apply some layer styles to it. This works in exactly the same way as it did with the text; open the Layer Styles palette and select one or many styles (here we've used a Wow Plastic style with a Wow Neon style edge).

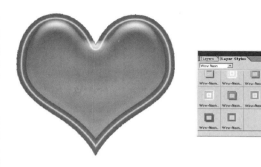

Our new shape, styles or not, now exists on the Layers palette and can be moved forwards or backwards as we see fit. Photoshop will consider all the areas without shapes on them as transparent.

Shape options

The other shapes all act in pretty much the same way. The Rectangular Shape tool draws rectangles (or squares with SHIFT held down); the Elliptical Shape tool draws ellipses or circles with SHIFT. Predictably the Rounded Rectangle tool draws rounded rectangles – we can specify the size of the rounding in pixels, though if we scale the object later, the corners will be scaled proportionally. This is similar to the Line tool (the width of which we must specify), or the Polygon tool (the number of sides we must specify).

All of the shapes also have various options dialogs, accessed using the pull-down triangle to the right of the various tools on the Options bar. The Unconstrained option is default, Square (or Circle on the elliptical version) is the equivalent of holding down the SHIFT key. Finally we can choose our own size as well, or some proportions to be fixed to. We need to type in (inches), cm (centimeters), or px (pixels) afterwards to specify the measurements.

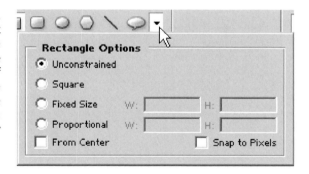

Creating new shapes

Trying to draw a more complicated shape – let's say a wrench – is all a matter of using the add and subtract buttons. Let's have a go:

1. We'll start with a new blank image, although it's possible to use a photo of our object as a background layer.

2. Next we draw a circle at the left-hand end of the image.

3. Then select the Subtract from shape area button from the Options bar.

4. To create our wrench's mouth we select the Polygon tool, type 6 into the Sides box on the Options Bar and then click somewhere off-center of the circle (the Polygon tool draws from the centre).

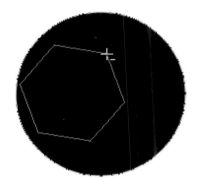

5. Next, we switch to the Shape Selection tool (to the far left of the tools on the Options bar) and click and drag a marquee over both shapes. We don't need to completely envelop both shapes – just so long as we get a bit of both of them.

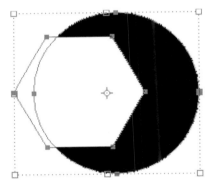

6. They will both become selected, as indicated by a dotted line and bounding box surrounding the outer limits of both shapes. We could use this bounding box like the Transform tool, to make it bigger, smaller or rotate it, but don't – for now.

7. If we click the Combine button to the right of the Options bar, Photoshop will now treat these too objects as one.

8. Next, we need to press CTRL/⌘+C and then afterwards CTRL/⌘+V – this makes a copy of our two shapes on the clipboard then pastes them in immediately above the originals.

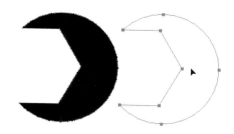

9. Holding down the SHIFT key, we can drag the new copy of our object off to the right. By holding down SHIFT, we only allow the object to move in horizontal, vertical or 45° planes, so that it will be at an even position with our original when we release it at the other end.

10. Again holding the SHIFT key to limit our options, we can rotate the new shape 180° then click the tick at the right of the Options Bar.

11. We now need to switch to the Rectangular Shape tool, and select the Add to shape area button on the Options bar.

12. To create the handle of our wrench, we need to draw a rectangle, starting inside the left head and finishing inside the right one. This time we don't simplify the shape layer.

13. The next thing to do is to bring up the Layer Styles palette and select the Shiny Edge texture from the Wow Chrome menu.

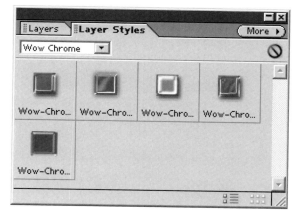

Although our wrench is drawn from two shapes (one of which was originally two), the chrome texture has only been applied to the outside edge. If we click on another layer, then the marker lines are removed (Photoshop does not print these).

Another thing we can now do (assuming we save as a Photoshop PSD file) is go back to that layer and make changes.

14. To make our wrench more realistic, we need to select the Shape Selection tool again.

15. If we then click on one of the ends of the wrench, we can rotate it as we see fit.

16. The final thing to do is to resize the whole image using the Image > Resize > Image Size... dialog. Notice here that we are increasing the resolution, something not normally recommended for photographs, as they tend to become blurry. This won't happen with our Photoshop file though – as all the effects are now recalculated for the larger size of our vector shapes.

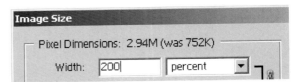

Color, brushes, filters, and effects

In this chapter

In this chapter we have a look at the things that don't really fit anywhere else. Things that we can do using the computer that we might not have expected, or needed! That includes the brush tools which, for the most part, should probably be considered just a bit of fun. We'll also turn our attention to the various filters available in Photoshop to change the texture and quality of our images, or areas of them. These vary wildly between the eminently practical and the entertaining. These are the topics we're going to cover in this chapter:

- ★ Color Picker
- ★ Brushes
- ★ Impressionist Brush
- ★ Filters – applying
- ★ Filters – handy effects
- ★ Filters – liquefy (alien faces)
- ★ Effects – snowstorm
- ★ Effects – borders
- ★ Aging an image

The Brush tool

Many of the tools in Photoshop require the use of various brushes, and in other chapters (if you followed them) we have already selected different sizes and types of brush head for use with the Selection Brush and the Clone Stamp tools. The approach here is much the same, though in reality the Brush tool might be regarded as the spiritual home of the other tools. Since the computer mouse was invented, there have always been programs allowing you to "draw" with it, by simply changing the color of the pixels under the pointer when you press the button. There is no change to the basic theory even now, though we have a much greater variety of styles and colors to choose from.

If it is so simple, why is it so far back in the book? Well, essentially because when we're editing photos, we're unlikely to have much use for the Brush tools. Because the Clone Stamp is the tool of choice when touching-up an image, it's unlikely we'll have an area of even enough color to touch up in a photo, unless we're aiming for an unrealistic effect. That said, the painting tools come into their own if used in the creation of original digital art, and of course, with digital art, we have the huge advantage of the Undo History palette – each brush stroke (that is, mouse click) is seperately recorded.

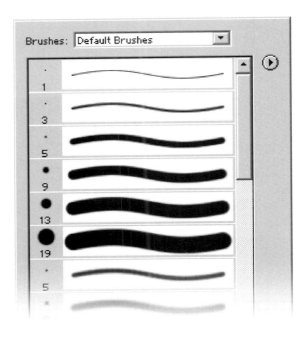

You can change the number of Undo steps remembered by going to the General Preferences *dialog and altering the figure of* History Steps.

Color pickers

The first step is to choose the color we are going to paint with, which will be the currently selected foreground color, shown at the bottom of the toolbar. Click on the foreground color to bring up the Color Picker dialog. This form of color selection is called Hue, Saturation, and Brightness – HSB – and it's not immediately obvious how to select a color, especially if the last time you made a color was with paints at nursery school! To choose a brown, we do this:

1. Work out what brown would be like with no black or white in it – an orangey color (trial and error is just as effective an approach).

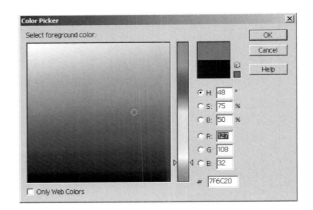

2. Move the Hue slider (click and hold on the rainbow strip) until the color we want becomes visible in the lager square. This slider is measured in degrees around the color wheel.

3. Now click on the color in the larger square. All possible permutations of the hue and saturation (how white the color is) and brightness (how black the color is) are represented. These are measured in percentages.

Alternatively, if our project is for the web, we can click on the Only Web Colors button in the bottom left of the Color Picker window. This limits our choice to the 216 colors that are certain to work on all computers on the Internet. This option, however, is becoming a little outdated as most installed machines now support more colors than this, and even those that don't, often have their own methods of dithering high-color graphics.

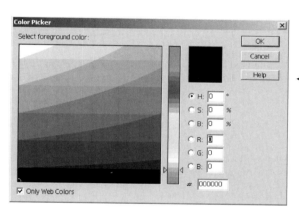

Also handy for web graphics is the ability to enter a color's RGB value in hexadecimal (the format preferred by web browsers and equivalent software) as well as the traditional decimal 0-255 values. If we know it we can simply click on the box(es) and type in the color we want.

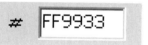

A final alternative is to use the operating system's default color picker. Simply go to Edit > Preferences > General and select the alternative to the Adobe version. Why you might want to do this is another matter – the Adobe HSB picker is probably the most intuitive of the lot, and the Windows one is horrible. Microsoft themselves rarely use it, and write alternative versions in their major packages, like the one you get when selecting a text color in Word XP. However, the choice is yours.

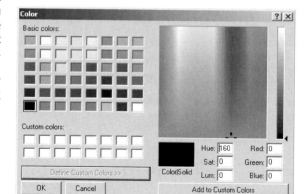

Also, don't forget the eyedropper tool, introduced in Chapter Zero.

Different brushes

On the right are just a few of the different preset brush strokes, to give an idea of the variety that the Brush tool offers. They all operate on variants of the same rules – when we click the mouse, a mark is made under the pointer.

Selecting brushes from the presets list is a relatively straightforward process – we just click on the Options bar where the currently selected style is shown and choose from the list – but there are a whole lot more options than that...

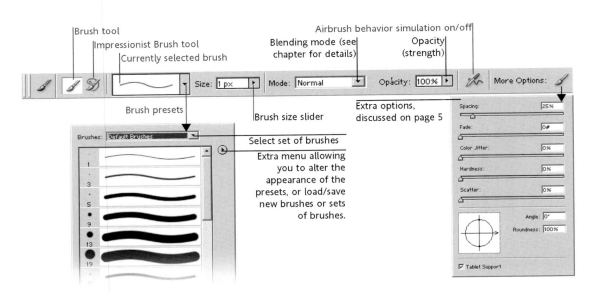

Brush tool

Impressionist Brush tool

Currently selected brush

Airbrush behavior simulation on/off

Blending mode (see chapter for details)

Opacity (strength)

Size: 1 px   Mode: Normal   Opacity: 100%   More Options:

Brush presets

Brush size slider

Extra options, discussed on page 5

Brushes: Default Brushes

Select set of brushes

Extra menu allowing you to alter the appearance of the presets, or load/save new brushes or sets of brushes.

Spacing: 25%
Fade: 0#
Color Jitter: 0%
Hardness: 0%
Scatter: 0%
Angle: 0°
Roundness: 100%

☑ Tablet Support

The presets have a lot of sizes included; the first six brushes on the menu here are the same circle, at widths of 1, 3, 5, 9, 13, and 19 pixels. Other sizes can be selected using the size slider in the Options bar.

We can also select the blending mode that the brush uses. You can learn more about blending modes in Chapter 3. As with Layers, we can adjust the opacity (how see-through the brush stroke is).

The airbrush simulation works by continuing to darken areas where the pointer comes to a rest but the mouse button is still held down, so is more obvious on soft-edged brushes. (This is as opposed to the phrase 'airbrushing' which is often used in the media as slang for a wide range of image manipulation techniques, especially those covered in Chapter 4.)

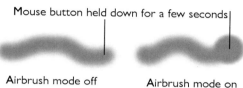

Mouse button held down for a few seconds

Airbrush mode off   Airbrush mode on

At the far end of the toolbar, the More Options button allows us to play around with all the possible permutations to our hearts' content.

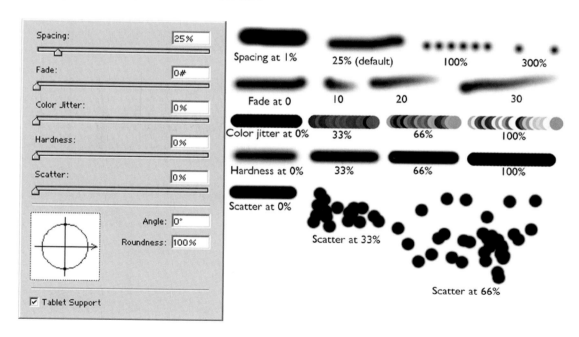

★ Spacing draws the brush shape at greater intervals apart. This defaults to 25%, not 1%, so as you can see with a soft-edged brush, closer spacing appears to darken the brush.

★ Fade set to 0# is off. At 1#, the brush fades out instantly, but at any other setting that number of dots are drawn. We can make this even more obvious by turning the Spacing up too.

★ Color Jitter alters the brightness (how near to white) of whatever our selected color is for each brush mark, at random. At 100% all shades up to white are used, at 10% then only shades up to 10% brighter are used.

★ Hardness effectively is the difference between a pure brush edge, at 100%, and a feathered one at 0%.

★ Scatter places each brush mark a random distance in a random direction from the pointer, the higher the percentage; the more the scatter.

And that, as they say, is all there is to it. If you're going to get into digital art, you've got all the tools you need. You've also got all the tools you need to change the color of your sister's face (and paint a witches hat on as well, now I come to think about it.)

The Impressionist brush

Of course we can't all be artistic, creative geniuses and in times of desperation we all know the best solution. Cheating. Which is why Photoshop also comes with the Impressionist Brush (Brush tool option). This might look very similar on the tool Options Bar, but it's job is to create something altogether different – impressionist masterpieces from our snaps.

Unlike the brushes above, the currently selected color has no bearing here. We just paint over an image we've already created, or loaded from another source. In the picture on the right, for example, a typical street scene has been partially scribbled over with the default Impressionist Brush.

Selecting a style works like this:

1. First, we select the style of brush that we want to make the individual brushstrokes in. This is essentially the interface we've seen for choosing a single brush style above.

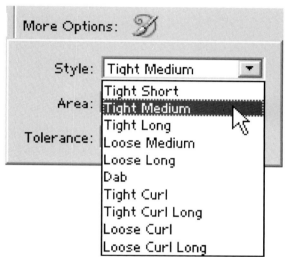

2. We can also select a mode (from a reduced list) and opacity as well.

3. Then we click the More Options button to choose the area of the overall Impressionist Brush (that is, the size of the area to which the smaller strokes that create the effect are applied), as well as a variety of styles. The different options in the Style dropdown refer to the length of each apparent brush stroke.

   The Tolerance option is off at 0, meaning that the Impressionist Brush will work on any color beneath it. At other percentages, it reduces the number of colors that the brush will act on. It will sample the color beneath the pointer when you start drawing, then only affect colors within your chosen percentage of that color.

The following picture gives some idea of the effects that the brushes are having on these shaded bars, but obviously you can't really experience them without trying them out on an image of your own.

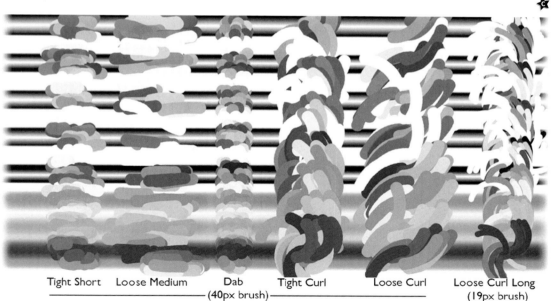

Tight Short	Loose Medium	Dab	Tight Curl	Loose Curl	Loose Curl Long

(40px brush) — (19px brush)

Filters

A topic touched upon in other areas of this book, especially with relation to blurring and sharpening, is filters. Filters are routines, typically mathematical in nature, applied to a whole image to achieve certain effects. In the olden days, graphic artists used these sparingly because computers took a long time to process them and they had to remember what they did by name alone. Luckily in Photoshop Elements, we've got things a little easier – all the filters, with little previews of their effects, have been put in the Filters palette, which we should whip out of the Palette Well now. (If you're in the business of nesting them, then its natural bedfellow is the Effects palette; more of that further on).

Using filters

As we can see from the palette, there are a huge variety of different filters – far too many for us to look at each one in detail here. The principles for each, however, are essentially the same, so we'll try making one of our pictures look more like a sketch, to give an idea of how they work:

1. Open the image that you wish to apply a filter too. For this example, we'll use the same street scene from earlier.

    A filter is only applied to one layer at a time, so if you're using an image with more than one layer, and want to include them in the same filter, you will have to flatten those layers.

2. Next, we need to open the Filters palette, and select the general category of filters under which the particular one we want falls. The categories are a handy way of locating a filter, if we can't remember the exact name.

3. Now we need to look through the palette for the filter we want. When we've spotted it, we simply pick it up with the mouse and drop it on the image (or double-click on it). For this example we're going to use the Chalk & Charcoal filter from the Sketch section.

4. We're then presented with a dialog box for the filter we've chosen, which allows us to adjust the settings of that filter. Filters typically work on a pixel-by-pixel basis; so many measurements given will be in pixels. The dialog should also have a preview of the final result – a small area of the whole so it is quick for the computer to calculate. We can move the preview around the image to see more important bits by clicking inside it and dragging.

5. In this case, let's try increasing the Stroke Pressure.

6. Remember, if we don't like any changes, we can easily reset any dialog by pressing ALT+Clicking on the Cancel/Reset button.

7. Finally, we click OK to apply the filter. Our final image is shown below:

Useful filters

In reality there probably are not too many occasions where we'd want to make our pictures look like this, but it's nice to know the option is there! Many more filters have more obviously useful effects, such as the Gaussian Blur filter for making photos look soft-focused, as discussed on page 243/4. Equally the Sharpen filters, if used in moderation, can occasionally help clarify images too.

For whatever purpose there's almost certainly a filter that's ideal, but the real problem is that they are essentially unintelligent, mathematical routines. They can't distinguish between a face and a car, just between colors and levels of contrast. For that reason, they're still a long way short of replacing human effort.

Liquify filter

A few of the filters don't behave quite as expected. While most bring up a dialog with an assortment of sliders and drop-down menus, the Liquefy filter in the Distort menu is a little special. Say your big brother, back from university (or any other victim) has earned your displeasure. The only sensible course of action, apart from stealing his glasses, is to turn him into the alien he undoubtedly is beneath his skin:

1. We'll start by going to the Filters palette, locating the Liquefy filter, which is in the Distort subset, and double clicking on it.

2. A new window will appear with the photo in the middle of an editing window like this. Along the left is a set of tools, which are switched between, in the same way as those in the main toolbar. On the right is a set of tool options for each tool on the left, and at the bottom-left is a zoom adjuster.

   The tools are all designed to help us stretch and misshape our image. We could use it to, say, make someone's hair wavy, or to be cruel...

3. To stretch something out, we need to select the Warp tool (). Let's say the middle of the nose is a good example. Suits him.

4. To make something go all wobbly – how about a jelly-neck – we can use the Turbulence tool ( ). This acts in a more random way than the Warp tool covered above.

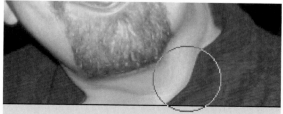

5. The Clockwise and Anticlockwise Twirl tools ( ) drag pixels around the brush's center point. That sorts out the ears nicely...

6. Like the two Twirl tools, the Bloat ( ) and Pucker ( ) tools also perform opposite functions – expanding and contracting areas (in this case both eyes) around the centre point of the brush.

7. The Shift Pixels tool ( ) can be used to move pixels around (holding the ALT key causes them to go in the opposite direction). The tool can be a little unpredictable, as it only works while the mouse is moving to exaggerate that effect. We've used it to give him a slightly bumpier skull!

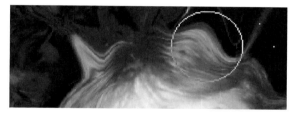

8. The Reflection tool (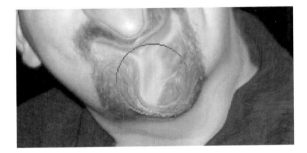) copies pixels from around the brush into the brush's center, as in the extension of the lips in this image. ALT+Clicking reverses the direction it gets the pixels from.

That's it for the regular tools, and there are plenty of opportunities for creativity here as well as cruelty. The other tool worth mentioning is the Reconstruct tool ( ) which works by gradually pushing pixels under the brush to their rightful homes, so we could, for example, restore the haircut. We can also undo one stroke with CTRL/⌘+Z.

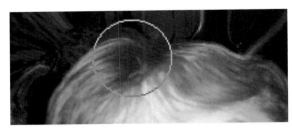

9. When we're happy with the changes, we just click OK and they're applied to the final image.

This is our last chance to get rid of the changes – we can click Undo now, or carry on and that image (or layer) will be permanently changed. In this case it rather suits him – perhaps he could help promote *The Lord of the Rings* films...

Effects

They might not seem it, but filters are limited in their scope. Their function is to move pixels around, and affect them, but it is a single step process. For years Photoshop enthusiasts have been putting a series of filters together, perhaps with steps of their own to produce a stylish result. In Photoshop 7, Elements' big brother, we can record these processes for ourselves, but in Elements we've been saved even the trouble of recording. A series of popular effects have been put together by Adobe in the Effects palette, which we can apply to our images.

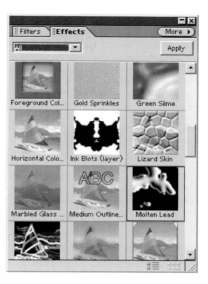

The process is very similar to using a filter – though not all of the effects are designed to work on an image. Some, like the Green Slime, simply add a layer of slime to the image! If we didn't know to turn down the opacity, we'd lose the picture altogether. Others, like the Frames, are little use without an image. The Text Effects all require a text layer to work, but leave a simplified pixel layer when complete.

Let's put some effects together to get a good final result...

1. For this example we're going to take this boring picture of a hotel and change the weather a bit.

2. We'll start by using the Effects palette to apply the Blizzard filter from the Image Effects submenu.

3. Notice how this has added a "blizzard" layer over the photo, with a Screen blending mode, so only the white parts (snow texture) show up. We can still select the photo layer and perform any alterations we might like, such as using the Brush to add some patches of snow.

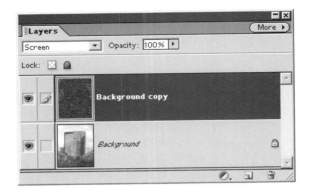

4. We can also make any other alterations we like, such as using the Clone Stamp tool to spread some of the darker clouds.

5. Although, if we were going for a real Christmassy effect there is one last step. Select the largest ellipse marquee possible around the new image, and then click Vignette (selection required) effect in the Frames subset. If we flatten our layers, we'll get the result on the right.

If you're looking for any sort of layer effect, or border to add to your image, then the Effects palette can be a goldmine. The textures can make particularly useful background layers. The white background behind the Vignette effect is only a layer, and any other color or texture could easily be used. Be adventurous, and remember, you can always undo!

Aging an image

Making a picture look convincingly old can take as long or as short a time as you want it to. Let's be believable but not go mad here – the in-depth approach would involve a great deal of worry about borders, but the important effects are the sepia toning and dust and scratches.

1. Start by opening your image, for this example we're going to use this image of Birmingham UK.

2. The first technique to apply is a Hue/Saturation adjustment layer to the background. For our example we've set the Hue to 38, the Saturation to 27. Remember to ensure the Colorize box in the bottom-right is checked. This will add our sepia tone (though we could use it to add any manner of tone if we wanted).

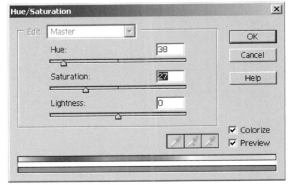

3. Next, we press CTRL/⌘+G to group the adjustment layer with the image underneath.

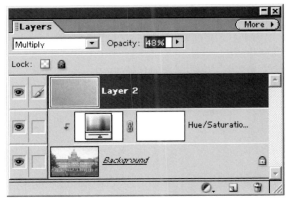

4. Now we need to give the image an aged texture. From the Effects palette we've selected the Gold Sprinkles texture.

5. Using the Blur subset of the Filters palette, we next apply a small Gaussian Blur to our new layer, choosing the level to create a suitably blotchy feel.

6. With that layer ready, we set its blend mode to Multiply and lower it's opacity to suit.

7. Now we need to create a new layer and make sure the layer is filled white rather than transparent. Do that by selecting the Paint Bucket tool and white as your Foreground color, then clicking anywhere on the layer.

8. With the new layer selected, we can add noise by clicking Filter > Noise > Add Noise..., or by using the Filters palette. For this example, we used roughly the settings pictured: Monochromatic, and Gaussian selected, Gaussian set to about 10.

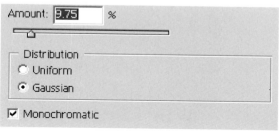

9. We then blur this layer too using Filter > Blur > Gaussian Blur set at 3 pixels.

10. Next we use Filter > Sharpen > Unsharp Mask at the maximum percentage setting, with a small Radius and zero Threshold.

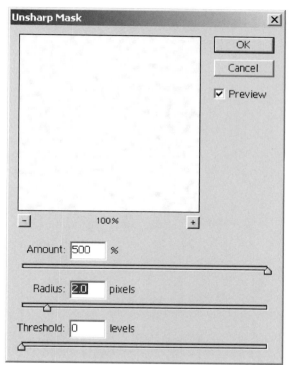

11. Now we do the clever bit – select Image > Adjustments > Threshold from the main menu. We are presented with a histogram and a slider. We can move the slider along until we get the amount of dust we want. The histogram represents the layers content like the one in the Levels dialog, but Threshold has only one slider – everything below it becomes black, everything above it becomes white. That has the effect of giving adjustable dirt levels.

12. Finally, we change the blending mode on the new dust layer to Multiply, so that all the color below shows through the white areas of our newly-created adjustable dirt layer. We can also reduce the layer's opacity ever so slightly, and get our final result.

The addition of the scratches and blotchiness makes quite a difference to what would otherwise just be one of a long line of sepia tone images. Of course there are further alterations that we might find appropriate too, like applying a grain filter (Filter > Texture > Grain), but these tend to imply something more specific than the passage of time.

Spot color

Finally in this chapter, a quick effect for those of you who have seen the film *Schindler's List*. In the above example, we saw the Hue/Saturation adjustment being used to 'colorize' an image, but it is also possible to apply the effect to individual parts of the color spectrum. You could use it, for example, to brighten certain colors, or, in this case, to reduce all colors except one specific group of colors:

1. Open an image. In this case, we're going to use this fantastic car.

2. Create a new Hue/Saturation adjustment layer by clicking on the circle icon at the bottom of the Layers palette.

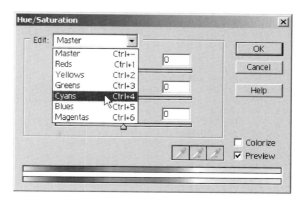

3. Unlike the sepia example we used, ensure that the Colorize button is *not* checked and, using the drop-down menu at the top, select a group of colors. In this case we want to affect all the groups *except* the red, so we'll start with its opposite – Cyan – and work from there.

4. You'll notice that two gray sliders now appear between the two spectrums at the bottom of the Hue/Saturation dialog. Remember that the spectrums really represent a circle of color – the cyan at either end 'loops' around. The darker gray area represents the area affected by our choices above.

5. Now click in the center of both gray sliders and drag them to either side of the red area of the spectrum. The dark gray now applies to almost the entire spectrum.

6. Now reduce the saturation of the selected areas of color. You can see exactly which colors you are affecting not only on the preview, but also on the lower spectrum in the dialog. It now only shows a red patch, with little tails beneath the light gray sliders. This is because the length of the gray sliders represents where our effect fades in and out.

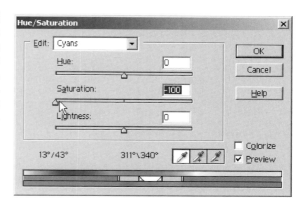

7. We can change the length by clicking and dragging the individual tiny end markers. In this case, we're going to shrink them so that the effect is more dramatic and really only get the reds, not the colors either side.

The final result is an image where only those things that were originally red (that is, the car) are picked out in red. The rest is in grayscale because we turned the saturation down to nothing. Other possible uses of this tool would be enhancing or reducing certain color tones, or creating crazy color shifts by adjusting the Hue of only certain colors.

Outputting your work

In this chapter

In this chapter, we'll be taking a look at the things that we can do to change the overall impression that our image gives. These are the topics we'll be covering:

- ★ Printing
- ★ Index prints
- ★ Picture package
- ★ Exporting files for the web
- ★ Saving for the web
- ★ Web galleries
- ★ Batch processing

Printing

This might seem like the most straightforward process in the whole program. However, printing from Photoshop Elements is a process filled with pitfalls, not least because getting it wrong can often be quite expensive if you're using good quality photo paper and pricey inkjet inks. In this section we'll have a little look at the things you need to check when you are printing your work to ensure that you get good results *first* time.

Simple printing

First things first: will your image fit on your page? There are a couple of things to bear in mind here, firstly the size of your image in Photoshop, and secondly any margins that your printer may impose. You can find out the size of your image in Photoshop as part of the printing process, and scale it to the page. The margins issue, however, is sometimes a little less scientific.

1. Open the Image you want to print.

2. Click File > Print Preview... or CTRL/⌘+P, which will bring up the Print Preview dialog. On the left is a representation of the page you are printing on, and how your image will appear on it. Its size is determined by the number of pixels and the image resolution.

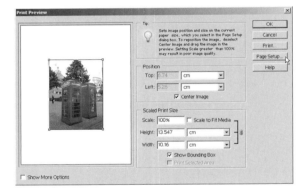

3. If you are using anything other than your printer's default paper type (typically letter/A4 plain paper) then you'll need to alter the Page Setup. Click on the Page Setup... button towards the top right.

4. This will bring up the Page Setup dialog allowing you to select the page size (from the list of sizes supported by your printer) and orientation. If your printer has more than one tray of paper, you can also select a different source.

5. If you are using a different paper type, or need to make any set up changes that only your printer software allows, you can click on the Printer... button in the bottom right-hand corner. This will bring up a dialog generated by your printer's own software, which depends on the manufacturer of your printer. They can often be quite complicated, but are the only way to select things like borderless printing modes, and printer quality settings, then click OK.

6. Check that your Page Setup options are still valid, then click OK.

7. Now we face a dilemma; we could either print the image at the specified resolution (that is, leaving the scale at 100%) – or we could scale it. You should make your decision based on how high the resolution of your printer is, and on how closely people will be inspecting the image. Here our image is at 300ppi, which makes it the Height and Width shown. The decision is yours.

8. If you don't want your image in the center of the page, uncheck the Center Image box and add your own dimensions.

9. When you are happy with your image's position on the page, click Print... (not OK) to print the image. If you click OK, all you have done is alter these settings, and will have to click File > Print > OK to actually produce the image.

This might seem a long way around the houses just to print an image, but there are a lot of things to ensure are correct; at the least we could waste some expensive paper. It is also quite tricky because your printer software acts as a gatekeeper in the process, and modern printers seem to come with a lot of options. It certainly wouldn't hurt to check the documentation that came with your

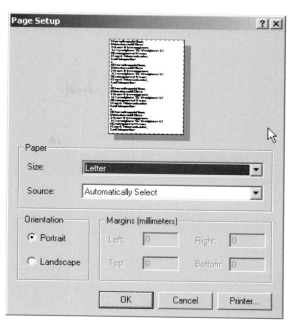

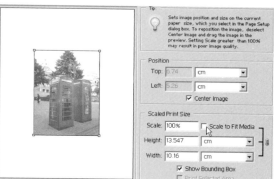

machine to see how to get the best results out of it.

Show More Options button

This button brings up an extra portion of the Print Preview dialog, which allows you to either apply a border to your image (from the Output subset) or play around with the color management. Given that color management is outside the scope of the book (because, most of the time, it is a waste of time and effort), and the Output options are incredibly simple to use, we'll leave out any in-depth discussion of them. Put simply, you can turn on and off things like a simple border for your image, or crop marks (trimming guides).

Index print

Sometimes, when you get your pictures back from the developers, they include an index print – a handy page of thumbnails not unlike Photoshop's File Browser. We can easily create one of these using Photoshop too, assuming all your images are stored in one folder (with or without subfolders) on your computer:

1. Click File > Print Layouts > Contact Sheet.... Contact Sheet is Adobe's name for this sort of sheet.

2. Select the folder of images that you want to use by clicking on the Browse... button at the top-left of the window.

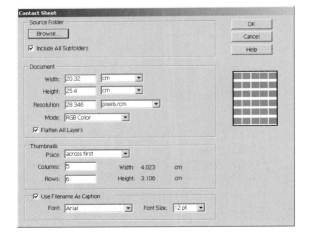

3. This will bring up a directory tree like the one in the File Browser; use the plusses and minuses to expand or collapse the tree, then click once on the name of the folder that contains your images, then click OK. These can be in any file format Photoshop can read.

4. Using the settings in the Document pane, of the Contact Sheet dialog, select the margins of your page. Although you should reduce these figures a little to allow for your printer's margins, here are some useful standards:

★ European A4: 21 by 29.7 cm
★ US Letter 8.5 by 11 inches

5. Set an appropriate resolution – if you're printing your page, you'll almost certainly want this to be nearer 200 or 300 pixels per inch, rather than the 72 default.

6. Unless you're printing on a black and white printer, select your Mode as RGB Color.

7. Also, unless you'll want to edit your page afterwards, ensure the Flatten All Layers option is checked.

8. The Thumbnails pane allows you to set the order the images are laid out on the page, using the Place options, and the number of Columns and Rows. Your choices are reflected by gray squares in the preview to the right, though if your pictures aren't the same shape, there may be more white space in the final version.

9. Finally you can choose to have the filename as a caption – very useful, though you might find a smaller font perfectly appropriate at a higher resolution.

10. Click OK and wait while Photoshop processes all the images to make little thumbnails and produce a new image – the contact sheet. This can take some time and is a lot of work for your computer.

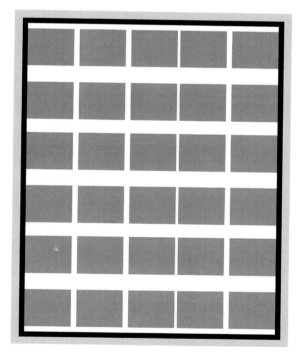

The resulting image is a normal Photoshop document, and a big file at that (a 300dpi letter sized page is around 60Mb). If you unchecked the Flatten All Layers option you can even edit the text (though you are left with a more unwieldy file). You can now print in the normal manner, as described on page 3.

Picture packages

Sometimes you want a lot of copies of the same image on one page, for example to cut out and give to your friends, and make a better use of expensive paper at the same time. Some film developers, for example, print three copies of one image on the same piece of paper, so it should come as no surprise that Photoshop will let us go one step further than that.

1. Open an image that you want to make into a Picture Package (although you can also open the image from the Picture Package dialog using the Browse... button).

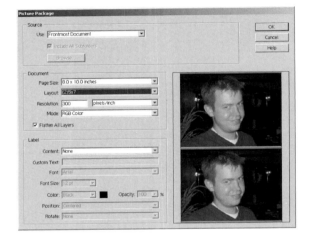

2. Picture packages are made using another slightly complicated dialog, but this time, we are looking for a single image. You can select this in the Source pane from three options:

   ★ Frontmost Document (which we'll choose) which uses the currently selected document.

   ★ File allows you to select a file from your computer disc using the Browse... button.

   ★ Folder allows you to select a whole batch of files, which Photoshop will do one after the other. Simply select a folder from the directory tree (though it's probably better not to ask for too many at once).

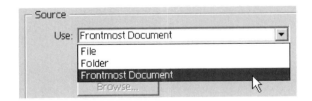

3. The Document pane allows you to select the final paper size, resolution, and color mode. If none of the page sizes on offer particularly suit you, remember that you can scale your image later in Photoshop.

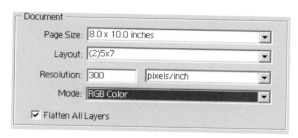

4. Also in the Document pane, we get to do perhaps the most important bit – select the layout of our page. The exact options available to you depend on which Page Size you've selected, but there are plenty of arrangements to choose from.

5. The Label pane allows you to add the same label somewhere on top of each of your images (not underneath, or to the side of). By default it is centered.

6. Finally, when we click OK we have to be prepared for a wait, as Photoshop then scales all the pictures one at a time (it's all a bit of a blur on screen, but it still takes its time).

Exporting images

Sometimes we want to use our images in other applications. Photoshop does have a huge range of features, but if we wanted to create a newsletter, or use our favorite word processor, then we're going to have to export our image. Exporting typically means saving in a non-native file format, where "native" means Photoshop's own PSD format. In reality, Photoshop regularly has to import a wide range of other image formats too, like JPEG (which most digital cameras take), so it's not quite the same thing here. Nevertheless there is one thing we can still be reasonably confident of, very few applications can cope with layered PSD files, so they'll need us to export the image:

1. Click File > Save As... (as opposed to Save). Unlike the ordinary save function, this method guarantees that we will be allowed to choose a new location for the file, as well as type, whereas Save will just save over the top of an older copy.

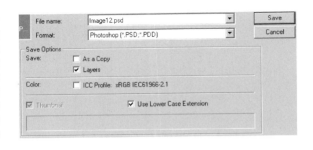

2. The layout here may depend on your operating system, but the principles remain the same. Using the File name box we can add our own name, and underneath we can select from a variety of file formats. It is worth checking what your target program supports, but good advice is to use JPEG to make a small file, for transmission over the Internet, and TIFF where the quality is important.

3. The Save Options at the bottom of the pane are less important. Saving As a Copy simply adds the word "copy" to the end of the filename (so it does not overwrite the previous version). Turning Layers off saves the image as a single layer, though most formats don't support layers anyway, and they do add unnecessary size to a file if we're exporting it. Either way, the options available to you in the bottom pane depend upon what file format you have selected.

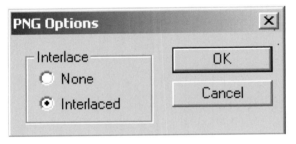

4. When you do save your file, you will almost certainly be asked more questions, in the form of file-type specific questions. These vary from the minimal, like PNG (a relatively recent format designed with the Internet in mind), which only has the one choice, to the more complex, like JPEG. JPEG file sizes depend on the quality at which you save them, and with the Preview option checked, Photoshop will calculate the eventual file size for you for any adjustments you care to make to the image quality.

When filling in these boxes, it pays to check the requirements of the program you will be using your file with. Sometimes a program can read some variants and not others, though you're unlikely to go wrong with JPEG or uncompressed TIFFs.

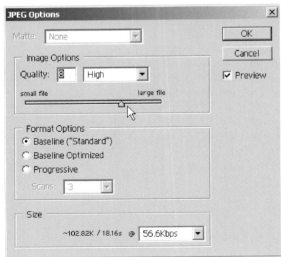

5. This time, when you click OK, the file is saved for you to do what you like with it. Common words for loading a picture into other programs are "Import", or "Place", and might be found on a menu called something like "File" or "Insert". If that program doesn't show your image at all, it might not recognize the file format.

Saving for the web

Exporting an image for a web page (or indeed any form of transmission by slow Internet connection – e.g. e-mail) is where file size really matters. On the plus side, with the web we have the worry of resolution taken away from us. All images on the Internet are supposed to be the standard for monitors everywhere – 72ppi. Photoshop can then greatly assist us in making that decision between poor and too poor:

1. Load your image and make any necessary crops – it would be a shame to have too much wasted space on an image on the internet.

2. Click File > Save for Web....

   The resulting dialog is much more complicated than the other save dialogs, and consists of some tools to the left of the main preview window, and a series of panes on the other side. There is also an extra menu accessed from the top-right of the preview area, which you can use to change advanced settings, like the assumed connection speed in the calculations at the bottom of the right-hand image preview.

   You can also turn Browser Dither on and off from that menu button – this simulates how images will look on older 8-bit (256 color) monitors using a web browser's dithering routine.

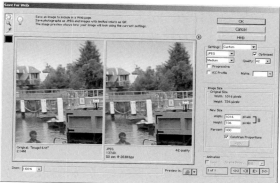

3. A sensible first step to apply to the image is to check it is the right size. In this case the pixel size is way too high for an Internet page, so we need to reduce it using the New Size pane to the middle-right. If we were using this image to illustrate a page of text, about a third of its original size might be appropriate.

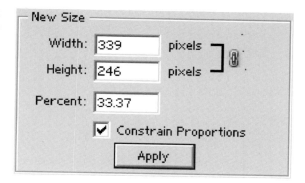

4. The next setting for the, image is to choose the file format. We are saving a picture, so we'll probably be best off with JPEG – it's main alternative on the web is better suited to graphics with a lot of solid color work. We can either select from a preset (at the top of the Settings pane), or choose our own settings using the individual pieces:

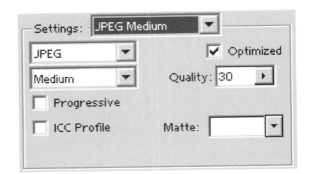

* ★ JPEG is the file format (the alternatives are GIF, or PNG 8 or PNG 24).

* ★ Medium is shorthand for the quality – on the opposite side a 0-100% quality slider can be used instead.

* ★ Checking the Progressive box typically adds to the size, and therefore the download time, but it means that the image appears to build up on the screen, so a lower quality version appears sooner.

* ★ Adding an ICC Profile theoretically improves the color rendering on those machines that understand them *and* are set up correctly, but adds file size.

* ★ Matte is the transparency color, and in JPEG can be used to select a background color to fill in transparent areas of your image.

Selecting the most appropriate quality is up to us, but here are the results at 0% (in the right hand window) and a few others below.

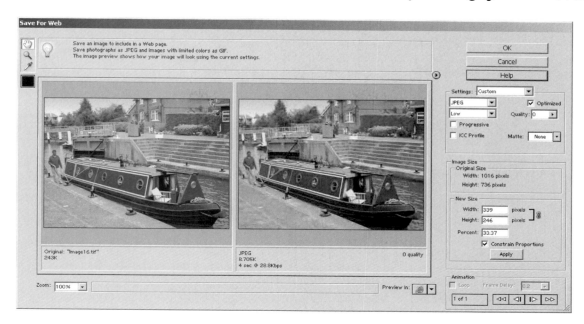

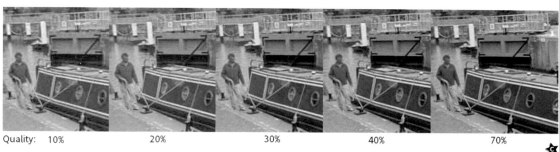

Quality:	10%	20%	30%	40%	70%

The apparent quality varies more at the lower levels, here, though the 10% quality image is around 11k, at 70% the image is 45k, so there is a big tradeoff for the cleaner lines. Anyway, the real point of this Save for Web... feature is that you get to choose exactly how good it looks, or how big it is. When you're happy, click OK to go through to pick a location.

Web gallery

Getting into the technicalities of publising on the Internet can be pretty complex, but there is another way. If your Internet firm has given you a bit of web space, you can have your family album up on the Internet in a matter of moments, all without a second of coding or even design. How?

Because Photoshop can prepare a gallery for you, scaling images all to a suitable size and doing all the HTML work. All you have to do is find somewhere to put it, and with most ISPs these days offering a small amount of web space, they can be available to the world (or at least those parts of it you give the address to) in moments:

1. Prepare a folder of images for your web site somewhere on your computer – pay particular attention to orientation (pics often come out the wrong way if you're lifitng them straight from a digital camera).

2. Click File > Create Web Photo Gallery....

3. You are presented with a quite daunting dialog box, which allows you to choose various styles for your web site, and add various personalizations. The first step is to select your style of site. Some of these have a lot of pre-prepared graphics for you, the others are plainer – the styles left over from Photoshop Elements 1 – but let you choose the color scheme yourself. These are:

   ★ Horizontal Frame
   ★ Simple
   ★ Vertical Frame

   Choose something that suits you. The preview gives you a clue – notice how some show the larger picture in the main window and have some thumbnails on the same page, whereas others feature a page of thumbnails leading to separate pages for your images.

4. Under the style, you may like to enter your e-mail address, which is included on the page by some of the styles. The Extension box is just to choose whether you prefer three or four letter file extensions on your HTML pages – best to leave it unless you have good reason to change it.

5. Selecting your folder is the same as elsewhere in this chapter, with the proviso that you will also need to select an output folder somewhere outside it to store your new web site before you upload it.

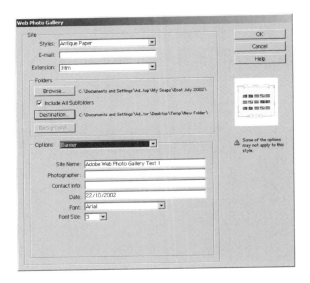

6. At the bottom (the Options pane) things get more complex, as there are now 5 panes to go through, making as many (or as few) changes as you want. These are fairly self-explanatory, but just so you know:

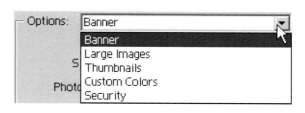

★ Banner – the names, your names, a site name etc, for the title page and the title bar.

★ Large Images allows you to set the maximum size of the larger images, as well as the level of compression involved. You can also choose what captioning to add to the images.

★ Thumbnails allows you to do the same for the thumbnails.

★ Custom Colors, if available, allows you to choose your own colors for fonts, background etc. These are unlikely to be available for the designed pages, but are handy for making the plain designs fit in with a color scheme of any site you already have.

★ Security allows you to add security (copyright) information, if you have included it with your images.

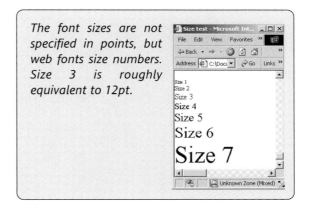

The font sizes are not specified in points, but web fonts size numbers. Size 3 is roughly equivalent to 12pt.

7. When you're happy with the changes you've made, click OK. Photoshop will get to work (it might take a few moments) creating a web site and putting it in the folder you specified. It will also open it in your default browser for you to inspect as soon as it is done.

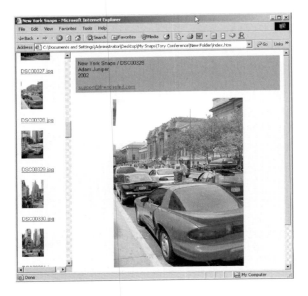 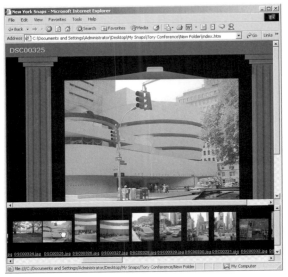

The example on the left is created using the Vertical Frame as specified, with colors selected in step 6. The example on the right uses (appropriately) the Museum style.

8. Uploading, however, can be a little more complicated. You will need to find out the exact details from your service provider. Typically this involves an FTP address (file transfer protocol) and a username/password. You can try typing the ftp address into Internet Explorer (if you use it) then waiting to be asked your username and password.

9. Use you filing system to copy the files from the folder Photoshop saved them in for you to this FTP site (drag them over), obeying any special instructions from your service provider. Your service provider will also let you know what your web address is.

Steps 8 and 9 are generalizations designed to show you how simple it is. We can't tell you your passwords though.

Batch processing

If you ever want to covert a whole batch of your images from one file type to another, or make them all matching sizes, then up until Photoshop Elements 2 came along it could be something of a chore. Now, mercifully, it has been tied together in one straightforward dialog.

As with so much in this chapter, it all depends on keeping images in certain folders and following the dialog through.

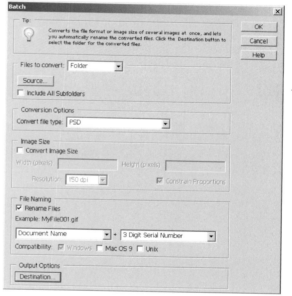

1. Specify the source – let's say a folder of images, or those open in Photoshop. The program will use any images in a file format it can understand.

2. Select a file type for your final image. This could be, say, JPEG (different quality options are available) so you can send a folder of images to someone.

3. If you check the Convert Image Size, you can specify a new size for all the images – the measurements are considered maximums unless you uncheck Constrain Proportions, in which case the image will expand in both directions.

4. If you select the Rename Files option, then the files will have logical names added by the computer, one after the other.

5. Don't check the Compatibility boxes if you don't need to – this just adds extra information (and size). Photoshop on Mac/Windows will read files from the other regardless of whether you tick this or not.

6. Finally, select a destination folder and click OK. Photoshop will get on with doing the boring opening, fiddling and saving for you.

Endgame

Admittedly this hasn't been the most exciting of chapters, but outputting your work is important because it's the only way you can share your results with others. In the last seven chapters we've seen almost all of Photoshop's features, but that isn't the end of the story. In the next half of this book, after the color section, we're going to take an in-depth look at a few different projects created using that vital last ingredient, creativity.

Enjoy....

Chapter Zero

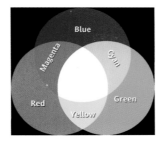 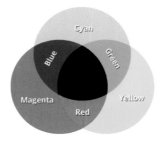

You probably already know that your computer monitor, like your television, mixes Red Green and Blue to produce every other color you see on the screen. This process is called **additive color**, as all three colors mix to create perfect white.

72dpi   300dpi

In it's simplest terms, the resolution of an image is its level of detail – the higher the resolution the better quality the image, but the larger the file size.

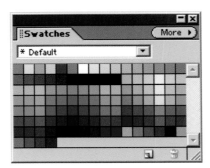

The Swatches palette is for those of us who find ourselves using color a lot.

Chapter 1

The other way of adjusting the levels is so quick it's barely worth mentioning – autolevels.

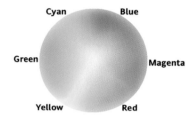

Color wheel

Chapter 2

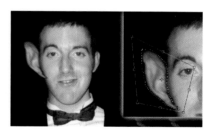

Chapter 3

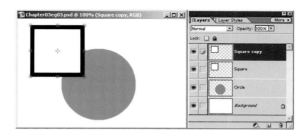

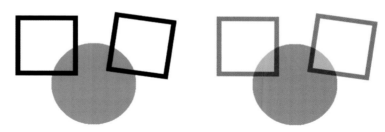

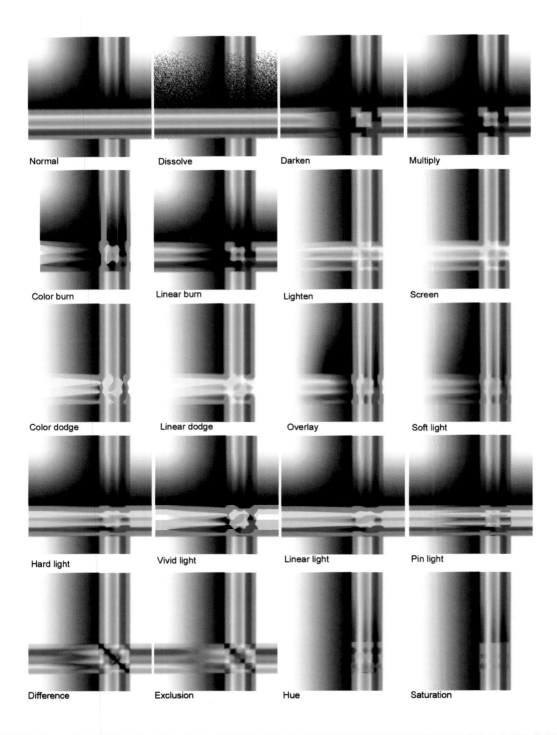

Normal

Dissolve

Darken

Multiply

Color burn

Linear burn

Lighten

Screen

Color dodge

Linear dodge

Overlay

Soft light

Hard light

Vivid light

Linear light

Pin light

Difference

Exclusion

Hue

Saturation

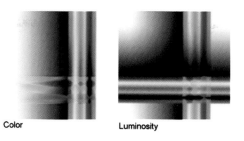

Color   Luminosity

Chapter 4

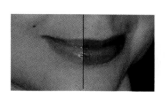

Chapter 5

Chapter 6

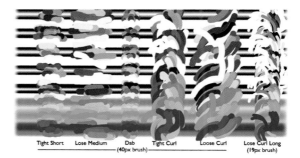

Tight Short   Lose Medium   Dab   Tight Curl   Loose Curl   Lose Curl Long
(40px brush)   (19px brush)

Chapter 7

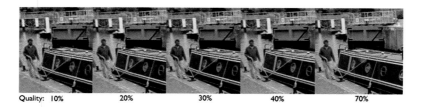

Quality: 10%   20%   30%   40%   70%

Graphic Design Techniques

In this chapter

In this chapter we're going to take a stock photo of the Eiffel Tower and turn it into a work of art that attempts to capture something of the romantic and exciting spirit of Paris, France, by night.

Our goal might be to commemorate a special memory with something a bit more permanent than a holiday snap; to create a card for a special occasion such as a birthday or anniversary; or to produce a promotional advert or poster to drum up business. Our ulterior motive is to really push Photoshop Elements to the limits; to discover just what we can achieve and how.

During the project we're going to be looking at all of the following:

- ★ Preparing your image
- ★ Basic image enhancement
- ★ Filter-based styling
- ★ Text handling
- ★ Style-based formatting
- ★ Layer-based compositing
- ★ Brush-based painting
- ★ Vector-based shape handling
- ★ Non-destructive color correction

Preparing the image

Our first task, as always, is to choose and prepare our starting image. If you are a keen digital camera user you might well have hundreds, even thousands, of images ready to go. If not, or if you can't find the perfect image to inspire you, then there are plenty of sources of good value stock images available on the Web. There is no shortage of starting material.

Choosing the best starter image is only the beginning. To make sure that you're off on the right foot you need to know that it's been saved to the most suitable file format. And right from the start of your project you have to think about your image's final output destination, which means thinking about its resolution. So let's see this put into practice.

One of the lesser-known secrets of Photoshop Elements is that it comes with a selection of free stock art images on the installation CD. If you've installed the Acrobat 5 Reader that is also included on the CD, you can view or print thumbnails of all the images by opening the Stock Art Catalog PDF.

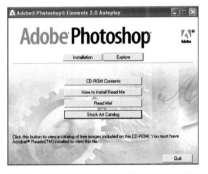

The stock images are designed to give you a head start on your own projects and to let you explore the power of Elements, so let's put one to good use. What we're looking for is a clearly recognizable subject with a good bold composition and a strong feeling or mood that we can pick up and enhance. The image that most fired our imagination was the picture of the Eiffel Tower by night.

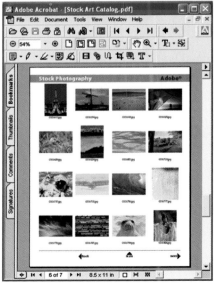

As with most photos from stock art collections or from digital cameras, the image simply has a numeric title – 0006613.jpg. We could make a note of this and then use Elements' Open dialog to navigate through to the right directory to access it. Instead we'll take advantage of Elements' ability to visually browse for images using the File Browser palette. To open this you need to select the File menu's Browse command (shortcut Ctrl/⌘+Shift+O) or click on the File Browser title in the Palette Well. Being able to see the images you are dealing with, rather than just their file names, makes a huge practical difference.

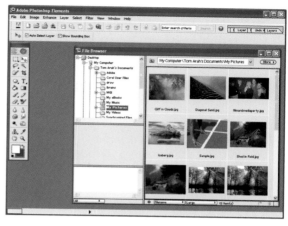

Next we have to use the directory tree down the left of the File Browser palette to find the CD drive and then to drill down through the Goodies directory to the Stock Art\Images directory. As soon as we do, the thumbnails of all supported file formats will quickly appear.

Using the scroll bar to the right of the palette we can scroll down until the Eiffel Tower image appears and then simply drag it onto a blank area of the main screen to open the file.

At the moment the image is stored on the CD which is a read-only medium so we immediately need to save it to the hard disk with the File > Save As command (shortcut Ctrl/⌘+Shift+S). For a project like this it's also a good idea to create a special directory to save the image in. That way, when we're experimenting later, we can save different versions while still keeping some sort of housekeeping control.

By default, Elements always saves an image in its current format, which in this case means the JPEG (Joint Photographic Experts Group) format. JPEG is one of the most important file standards as it's amazingly efficient and enables large photos to be saved to reasonably small file sizes – that's why it's the most common format for digital camera, web and stock art images.

However, JPEG has a serious downside – it's "lossy". This means that each time that you save and open your image as a JPEG the quality deteriorates and detail is lost that you can never get back. As we're going to be working heavily on this image, we need to save to another format.

The most common format for lossless compression of flat images is the TIFF format but, as we're going to be producing a layered photo-montage, the best option is to save to Photoshop Elements' native format – PSD. And at the same time let's give the image a meaningful name – `paris.psd`.

We've just saved our image for the first time, but now's the time to think about our final output options. If we call up the Image > Resize > Image Size dialog we can see that our image looks pretty large at either 38.8cm x 26.1cm or 15.3 x 10.3 inches depending on which unit of measurement you choose. At this size our image looks like it would be more than large enough to fill a sheet of Letter or A4 sized paper.

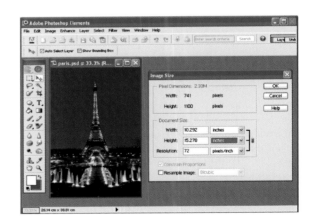

Sadly this is entirely misleading. The problem is the resolution setting which is set to just 72 pixels per inch (ppi). If we printed the image at its current size at such a low resolution the results would look hopelessly soft and blurred and we might even be able to distinguish individual pixels - the dreaded pixelation.

In fact what really determines the realistic maximum output size is a combination of the image's pixel dimensions, which in this case is 741 pixels by 1100 pixels, and the resolution of your *output* device. If you were producing an image for a typeset coffee table book, for example, you'd ideally be looking for 300 pixels per inch. To see what this means for output size we can switch the Resample Image option off and change the resolution setting to 300ppi. When we do, the image dimensions automatically update to show the new output size of just about 2.5" x 3.5" or 6.3cm x 9.3cm

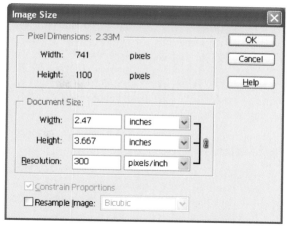

Clearly we just don't have enough pixels to produce a large poster for commercial print. But surely we can increase our image's pixel dimensions to anything we want right here in this dialog? If we now make sure that the Resample option at the bottom of the dialog is set to On, we can increase both width and height by 400 percent and then hit OK and this time Elements will automatically add the appropriate new pixel information.

Look at the resulting image, however, and it's immediately clear that our enlarged image is unusably soft and strongly pixelated. We better hit Edit > Undo (shortcut CTRL/⌘+ALT+Z) immediately to return to our original image. The important lesson to understand here is that you can't produce detail that wasn't there in the original image - you really need to make sure that your source image has enough pixels before you start.

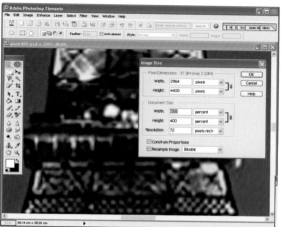

However that's not always an option, and isn't in this case, so we need to make the most of what pixels we've got. Let's reopen the Image Size dialog and this time set the resolution to 150 pixels per inch which is a compromise between our original 72ppi and the maximum 300ppi and which should produce acceptable results on a local inkjet printer. This time we're only changing our image's default output size, not its actual pixel information, so we need to make sure that the Resample option is set back to Off. When we do, the Width and Height settings automatically update to reflect the much more reasonable new output size of 4.9" by 7.3" or 12.6cm by 18.6cm.

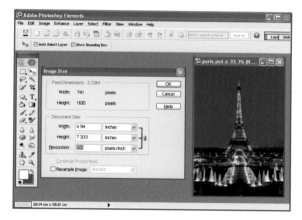

We could resample to increase this figure slightly, say by a factor of 1.5, without the quality degrading too badly, but for the moment let's just accept the pixels that we've been given. We might not have enough to produce a commercially printed poster, but we've certainly got enough to produce an advert or an anniversary card - and to put Elements through its paces.

Basic image enhancement

The next step with our image is to enhance it. This is a professional stock photograph so already of high quality and we're soon going to be giving it a radical, artistic makeover, so it's not worth putting too much effort into advanced color correction. However, with a couple of quick steps we can still do a lot to make the image better suit our purposes.

To begin with, as a night-time view, the image is naturally very dark with its tonal range heavily biased towards the shadows. Applying the one-off Enhance > Auto Levels command (shortcut CTRL/⌘ +SHIFT+L) means that Elements automatically increases the image's tonal range by identifying the lightest and darkest pixel in each of the image's red, green and blue channels and stretching them across the maximum 256 possible levels.

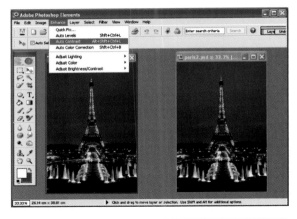

The Auto Levels command helps bring out the image's tonal range but in this case introduces a color cast, turning the sky from a near-black to a dark blue. In some cases this color change would be undesirable (in which case the Auto Contrast command would be a better option) but in this case it makes the sky look less forbidding and more attractive so we'll stick with it. In fact we'll go further by calling up the Enhance > Levels dialog (shortcut CTRL/⌘ +L) and moving the middle input slider under the image to the left. This has the effect of further stretching out and lightening the mid-tones of the image while leaving the strongest shadows and highlights unchanged (this is preferable to the relatively crude and linear Brightness/Contrast command). This way we keep

the benefits of the spectacular lights on the tower while the sky becomes less looming and more inviting.

Filter-based styling

Thanks to Elements' core enhancement capabilities, our image now has more tonal range and color to work with which we can now put to good use by exploring Photoshop Elements' special effects filters.

Over the last decade Adobe has built up a wide range of over 100 filters for use in its top-of-the-range Photoshop application – and all of these are available to us via Elements' Filters menu. The effects are divided into groupings and, as we're interested in giving our image an art feel, we're mainly interested in the filters in the Artistic and Brush Strokes categories and, to a lesser extent, the two-tone effects in the Sketch category.

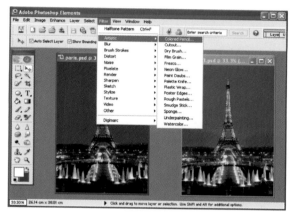

This means there are around forty effects to explore so it's fortunate that Elements makes the job easier for us with its Filters palette (available from the Window > Filters command or via the Palette Well). The main advantage of the palette is that it shows thumbnails of the sort of results that can be achieved with each effect so that you don't waste time trying effects that you wouldn't like. It also has the added bonus that, using the dropdown at the top of the palette, you can choose to see all filters simultaneously.

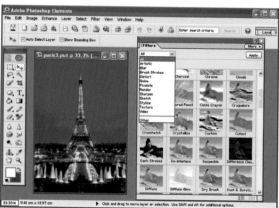

Selecting a command from the Filters menu or double-clicking on a Filters palette thumbnail calls up dedicated dialogs in which you can set the parameters for each effect. Crucially, each dialog also displays a small thumbnail preview of the current image with the current effect applied to it, which very quickly gives you an idea of whether it's worth fine-tuning the parameters (you can also pan and zoom the preview to get a better idea). Here we've accepted the defaults for the Dry Brush effect.

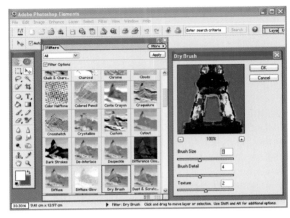

Photoshop Elements' built-in filters are impressive but you'll often find that, on their own, they won't quite give the overall effect that you're looking for. What you really want is a part of one effect and a touch of another. If that's the case then there's nothing to stop you from applying one filter after another to produce your own customized artistic effect. Here for example we've followed up the Dry Brush filter with the Fresco filter which produces a very nice, almost Van Gogh-like effect.

When you're exploring filters in this way Elements' Undo History palette really comes into its own. Using it you can follow one path to see where it leads you but, if it leads to a dead-end, you can always backtrack to any earlier stage and begin exploring again. The Image > Duplicate Image command is also extremely useful here as it enables you to save a snapshot of the current state of the image as a separate file while you backtrack to explore other possibilities.

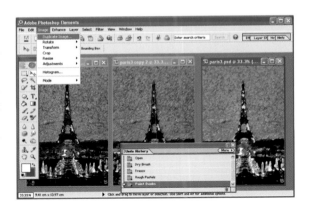

Combining filters with the flexibility offered by the Undo History command opens up a lot of options, but Elements has another capability which really takes your creative possibilities onto a new level. The secret is to make use of the Layers palette (shortcut F11). You can copy a version of your original image to a new layer simply by selecting it with the Select > All command (shortcut CTRL/⌘+A) and then copying it (shortcut CTRL/⌘+C) and pasting it (CTRL/⌘+V). You can then explore different filter effects on the new layer which automatically obscures all layers below. Here for example we've applied the Watercolor effect.

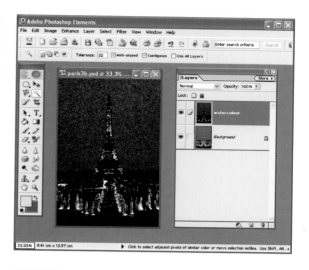

Working with layers like this is often more convenient than trying to handle multiple image versions, but the real beauty of the approach is that it lets you seamlessly mix effects by varying their apparent strength. Here, for example, the watercolour effect is too overpowering on its own, but by lowering the layer's Opacity with the slider at the top of the Layers palette you can lighten the effect and merge it into the realistic photographic background.

More than this, you can change the blending mode, which affects how each pixel's values combine with those below (the effect of some blending modes such as Darken are self-explanatory but generally your best bet is just to experiment to see their effect). In this case, for example, changing the blending mode to Pin Light produces a completely new crossover effect.

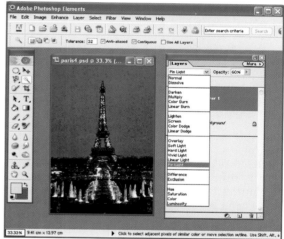

By mixing layers, filters, opacity and blending modes the number of possible creative effects is near endless. However, if you still can't find the effect you are after, Elements has another ace up its sleeve – support for third-party filters. Over the years literally thousands of different plug-ins have been developed to work with the market leader, Photoshop, and, thanks to Elements core tie-in with Photoshop, all of these will work with Elements.

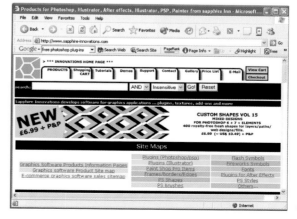

Of course some sets of professional filters will cost more than Elements itself but others, such as those from Sapphire Innovations (www.sapphire-innovations.com), are very reasonably priced. Even better you'll find that many sites give away free sample plug-ins. They might be a bit rough around the edges but they could just give your work the edge it needs.

One budget set of filters that we are particularly fond of and which fits in perfectly with the art-based feel we are looking for is Virtual Painter. There's an evaluation version available from www.jasc.com and if you decide to buy it, it costs just US$45.

Once you've installed any plug-in filters, you access them from the Filters menu just as you do with Photoshop's in-built effects. In the case of Virtual Painter this takes the form of eight effects ranging from Collage through to Watercolor and are all designed to produce results that mimic traditional artistic approaches.

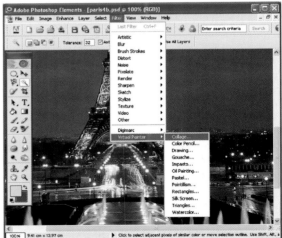

After exploring each of the effects, there's one that really caught our eye – Collage. What makes it stand out is the way that it seems to act much more like a real human artist, not just laying down patches of strong flat color but pulling out the lines in the image and redrawing them with a flamboyant flourish. It's instant artistic flair and really does give our image a hand-drawn feel. Not bad for a couple of clicks.

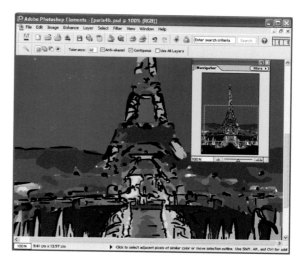

Text handling

We've got the most important element of our image, the background canvas, exactly the way we want it; now we can begin to embellish it. And the first thing we want to add is an eye-catching message.

Before we can add the text though, we've got a small problem. We don't want the text to interfere with the central composition by obscuring the tower, but there's not quite enough space above. In fact we can easily work our way around this using the Image > Resize > Canvas Size command to make more room. The new canvas added will automatically pick up the current background color so we need to set this first by double-clicking on the background swatch at the bottom of the toolbox. When the Color Picker is open, moving the cursor over the image turns it into the Eyedropper tool so we can simply click on the sky to set the background color to the existing dark blue. (We're extremely lucky here as the fact that our sky is a single flat color makes life very simple.)

We're now ready to call up the Canvas Size dialog. Because we only want the canvas added to the top of the image we need to set the anchor at the bottom of the dialog and then type in the new desired height. Click OK and we've got enough room to add our text.

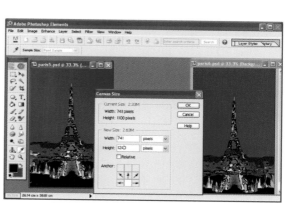

To add our title, "Paris", we need to select the Text tool and then, from the drop-down list in the context-sensitive property bar, choose an appropriate font. We're looking for a fluid hand-drawn feel in keeping with our poster-style and we particularly like a font we just happen to have on our system called Smudger LET as it's strong, friendly and there's just a hint of Toulouse Lautrec about it.

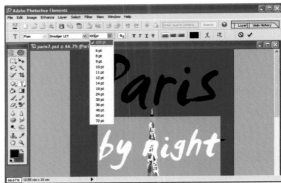

To add the second line, "by night", we can just click below the main title and begin typing. By default, the type picks up the previous formatting which is too large for the subheading. We can shrink the text by selecting it (shortcut CTRL/⌘+A), changing the size in the property bar and then, when we're happy, simply clicking on the Commit command at the end of the property bar or by pressing ENTER.

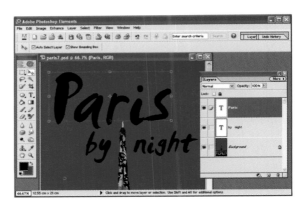

If we open the Layers palette we'll see that each line of text has automatically been added on its own separate layer (also notice that the layers are automatically labeled). These layers are clearly marked as special type layers and the big difference to the pixel-based image layers that we saw in action earlier is that they are vector-based. This has a big advantage in that if you select Type layer with the Move tool (shortcut V), not only can you drag your text into position but you can use the surrounding bounding box to quickly resize and rotate the layers. And because the text is stored as vectors, no matter how you transform your type it will remain absolutely pin-sharp.

Thanks to Elements vector text handling, it's a matter of moments to resize and drag our text into a pleasing arrangement with the main "Paris" title almost impaled on the tower and the "by night" strapline cut in two by it.

The other advantage of vector, compared to pixel-based handling, is that the text remains completely editable. To go back and change our existing text all we need to do is select the desired layer and click on its text with the Type tool. In this case it's particularly useful as it means that we can go back to add extra spaces between the two words "by" and "night" to ensure that they don't obscure or interfere with the tower.

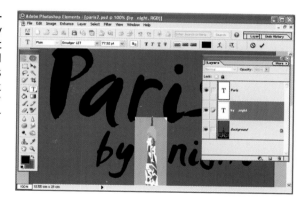

While our text is selected, we can also change its color. Clicking on the color swatch in the Text Property bar calls up the same Color Picker that we saw earlier. We could specify any color we wanted by dragging on the color slider and clicking within the color field, but it's more in keeping with the limited palette of our poster-style look-and-feel to stick to an existing color. By moving the cursor over the image we can again use the Eyedropper tool to pick up an existing color from the tower. This will also subliminally help to tie the text in with the rest of the image.

Style-based formatting

Colouring our text makes a big difference, but it still seems a bit flat. To make it really stand out we can take advantage of Elements' layer-based formatting available from the Layer Styles palette (itself available from either the Palette Well or the Window menu or the F9 shortcut).

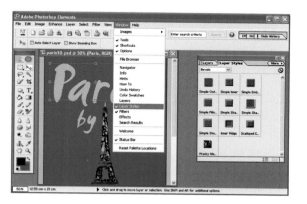

The most obvious way of giving our text a lift is to select the Drop Shadow option from the palette's drop-down menu of style categories and then to experiment with the options provided. Each layer can only have one drop shadow effect so that you can simply click on each in turn to see which one looks best. In this case the Noisy option looks more artistic and as if it has been sprayed on by hand with an airbrush, so we'll go with that for both text layers.

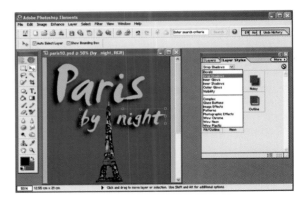

At first it looks like we don't have any customizable control over the effects but in fact it's just hidden away. If you open the Layers palette you'll see that each layer with an associated layer style is indicated with a lower case "f" symbol (standing for "effect"). Clicking on this symbol calls up the Style Settings dialog where you can set the Lighting Angle and the Shadow Distance for the drop shadow. And notice that, because the Use Global Light option is set to on by default, if you change the Lighting Angle this automatically updates both text layers so that they seem to be lit by the same source.

You can only apply one drop shadow effect to each layer but you can combine different layer styles from different categories. For our main 'Paris' title, for example, we can compliment the noisy drop shadow effect with the Simple Noisy option from the Inner Glow effects.

So far we've been applying the same effects to both text layers, but now it's time to give the sub-heading a distinct identity of its own. Rather than applying the same Inner Glow, let's explore our other options. As we're trying to emphasize Paris's exciting night-life the effects in the Wow Neon category are an obvious temptation.

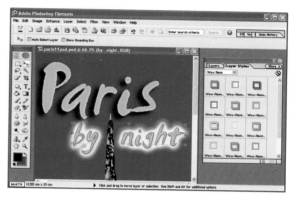

In the end they prove just too overpowering, so instead let's choose a textured fill effect from the Pattern category. Many of these, such as the rainbow-colored Nebula effect, are spectacular but in the end we chose the silvery Brushed Metal look as it gives the text a subtler, almost moonlit feel. The end result gives the subheading an identity of its own but without competing with the main title or unbalancing our overall design.

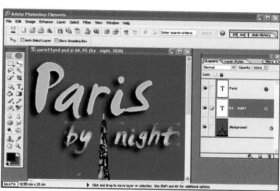

Layer-based compositing

The moonlit effect on our text is a good start but we've still got a long way to go to give our overall image that romantic late-night feel. The major problem is the sky. The current twilight blue is attractive but it's a solid flat color and there's just too much of it.

This gives us the perfect opportunity to see layer-based compositing, one of the most common tricks of the Photoshop professional, in action. By isolating the sky and copying it to its own layer we can edit it without affecting the underlying image. The creative flexibility layer compositing opens up is enormous and the big benefit of this approach is that, if we don't like the results, we can simply delete the layer and no harm has been done.

★ Hero

Our first job is to create our selection. To do this we have to make sure that the background layer is selected and then choose the best option from Photoshop Elements' many Selection tools. Again the fact that we are dealing with an artistic image with a limited palette is a great help here. In fact, because the sky is a single flat color we simply need to click on it with the Magic Wand tool. That leaves two patches of sky unselected within the tower but these can be added to the current selection by SHIFT+clicking on them (or by setting the current tool mode to Add to Selection in the Options bar).

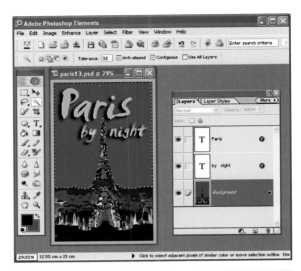

Now that the selection has been made, we can convert it into a new layer with the Layer > New > Layer via Copy command or simply by copying (shortcut CTRL/⌘+C) and then pasting (shortcut CTRL/⌘+V).

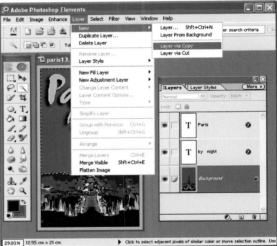

By default the layer is simply labeled as "Layer 1" but to avoid getting confused, particularly on larger projects, it's always a good idea to give the layer a meaningful name. This is easily done by double-clicking on the layer in the Layers palette to call up the Layer Properties dialog.

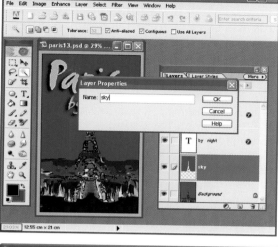

We now need to reselect the sky on this new layer which is easily done by CTRL/⌘+clicking on the layer name in the Layers palette. Now that the sky is selected we could change its color by clicking on it with the Paint Bucket Tool (shortcut K) or even get Photoshop Elements to automatically generate a cloudy effect with the Filter > Render > Clouds command.

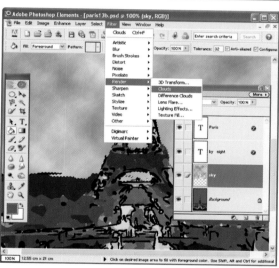

It's a nice effect but hardly in keeping with either our artistic feel or night sky theme. A much better idea is to add a simple but strong gradient to the sky from pitch black at the top of the layer down to the existing blue at the bottom. One way to do this would be by setting black as the foreground color and the blue as the background and then dragging on the sky with the Gradient tool (shortcut G). Instead let's take advantage of another of Elements' great strengths, the use of non-destructive Fill Layers, by making sure that the Sky layer is selected and then calling up the Layers > New Fill Layer > Gradient command.

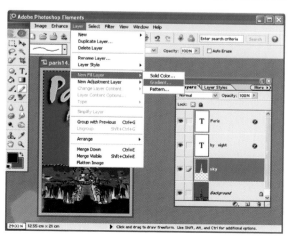

This calls up the Gradient Fill dialog. If it's not already selected, we can choose the default linear gradient between solid black and transparent from the drop-down list at the top of the dialog ready to be overlaid over our existing blue sky. Let's just accept these defaults and click OK and in the Layers palette you'll see that a new Fill Layer is automatically added complete with a layer mask corresponding to the currently selected sky. (If the sky wasn't selected the gradient would cover the entire image.)

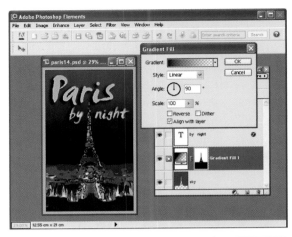

That's great - except that the gradient is upside down for our purposes. Fortunately it's no problem as the beauty of Fill Layers is that, like Layer Styles, they are non-destructive and so remain fully editable. All we need to do is double-click on the Fill Layer thumbnail preview in the Layers palette. The Gradient Fill dialog reappears ready for fine-tuning which in this case involves changing the Angle of the effect or, even more easily, simply select the Reverse option. The end result is not only more naturalistic it also gives us the best of both worlds: the darkness at the top of the image is more romantic while the original blue at the bottom suggests the excitement of the vibrant city lights.

Brush-based painting

Our night sky is certainly striking but it's still essentially empty and crying out for a bit of action. An obvious idea, that manages to be both romantic and exciting at the same time, is to add some fireworks. And that gives us the opportunity to see Elements' brushes in action.

The first step, as you might guess by now, is to add a new layer either with the Create New Layer icon at the bottom of the Layers palette or with the Layer > New > Layer command (shortcut CTRL/⌘+SHIFT+N), and to label it "fireworks".

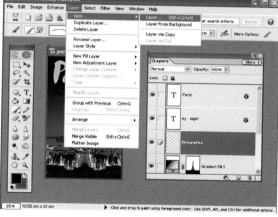

Next, after selecting the Brush tool (shortcut B), we have to choose a brush from the drop-down list on the property bar. Most of Elements' brushes are round but, down at the bottom of the list, you'll find some more exciting variations. The one we are looking for, "Flowing Stars", is based on a scattered star-shaped dab which is perfect for the job.

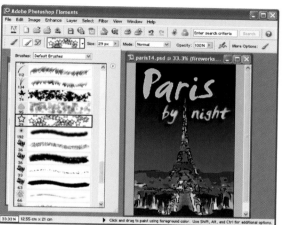

Before painting we want to set the foreground color of the stars to white so that they stand out against the sky. The easiest way to do this is to use the two icons next to the color swatches in the toolbox. The first restores Element's Default colors of black and white (shortcut D) while the second switches the Foreground and Background colors (shortcut X). We can then draw an arc of stars to represent the fireworks exploding in the night sky.

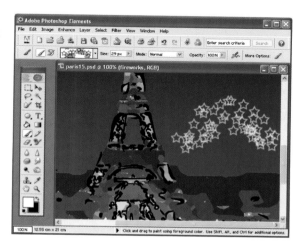

★ Hero

The scattered and overlapping stars look the part - but they are too regular and dull. What we need is some color-based excitement. That's no problem as we can apply layer styles to pixel-based layers just as we did to type layers. And the obvious solution for producing a multi-colored fireworks-style effect is to turn to the Nebula pattern that we noticed earlier.

It's a huge improvement but we've lost some of the immediate impact of the white. To remedy this we can simply create another layer, "fireworks 2", and this time, by clicking rather than dragging, we can add single white stars wherever we feel they are needed.

Now we need to add the firework trails so again we need to create a new layer, "fireworks 3" and select a new brush. This time let's select a more traditional round brush with a soft edge.

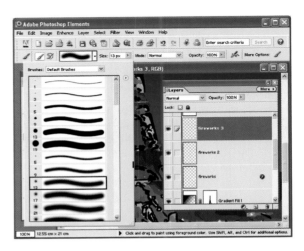

By itself this brush would still look too hard and not in keeping with our illustrated feel, so before painting we also want to use the property bar to change the opacity to 50% and the blending mode to Dissolve. When we paint on the strokes of the fireworks' trails we can see how this produces a much more grainy effect more like charcoal or a trail of sparks.

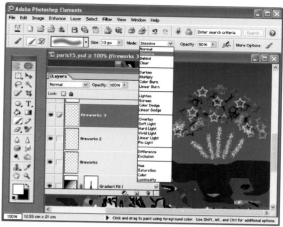

Finally we can fine-tune our effect. We can paint out unwanted lines or stars using the Eraser tool (shortcut E) and, because we've used layers, we can easily reposition and resize the three different elements of our fireworks effect and change their opacity and blending mode.

Finally, when we're completely happy, it's a good idea to link the three layers by clicking in the second column between the eye symbols and layer names in the Layer palettes, as this means that the fireworks can be treated as a single unit if we need to reposition or resize them later.

Vector-based shape handling

The fireworks certainly add some excitement and glamour to our image, but it's all rather distant and abstract - there's very little sense of human involvement in the image and we haven't got over the idea of travel. The obvious way to help the end viewers to imagine themselves in the Paris nightscape that we've created is to add a plane. Painting a realistic plane would be quite a challenge for most users' artistic capabilities but Elements provides us with the perfect solution - and in the process gives us the opportunity to see the benefits of vector-based shape handling in action.

★ Hero

The first thing we need to do is to select the Custom Shape tool and to explore what Elements has to offer. To begin with, this looks less than promising as the default set of thirty shapes is very limited. However, by clicking on the preset dropdown's fly-out menu, we can load more images. Much the easiest option is to load them all.

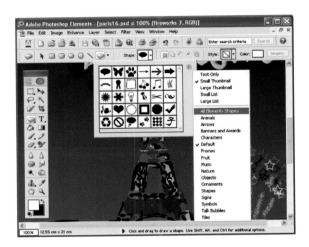

And towards the middle of the full selection are a range of transport-themed symbols including several of planes. Let's pick the most realistic one.

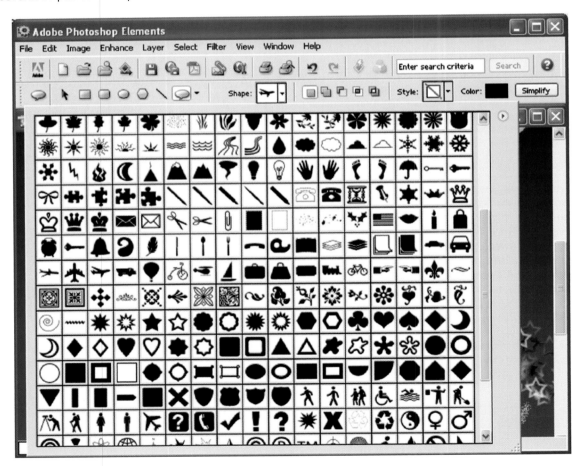

Next we need to make sure that our shape color is set to black on the property bar and then we can drag on the screen to add the plane (holding down SHIFT at the same time ensures that the aspect ratio of the original is maintained). Elements automatically creates a new layer which it calls "Shape 1" but which we can rename as "plane".

At the moment the plane looks as if it is about to crash into the tower so let's move it safely onto the right side of the image with the Move tool (shortcut V). That means that there's a lot happening on the right of the image so let's add another shape on the left to restore some balance. The hot air balloon is the perfect choice as again it adds human interest, suggests travel and adds to the romantic feel and at the same time reminds us of Paris's great history.

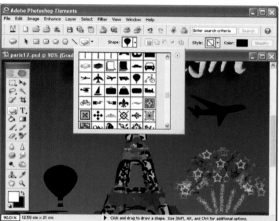

Another shape is just crying out to be added to our montage – namely the crescent moon. By default the moon is pointing to the left and so leads the eye away from the image, but it's simple to drag the shape's vector bounding box so that it's facing into the picture. We can also open the Layer Styles palette and apply the same Brushed Metal look that we earlier applied to our "by night" subheading.

And of course if the moon is out you'll expect to see some stars and again there are a couple of vector-based shapes to make life easy for us available in the Custom Shape drop-down. Let's choose the hollow five-cornered option as it ties in with the brush we used earlier to paint the fireworks. And to help integrate the image even further, let's apply the same Nebula pattern-based layer style.

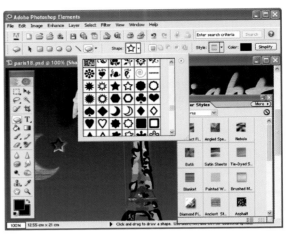

If we take a look at the Layers palette we can see how each of the shapes we've added has automatically been added on its own layer. These layers have been automatically labeled "Shape 2" and so on, but it will be much easier to manage them if we give them meaningful names.

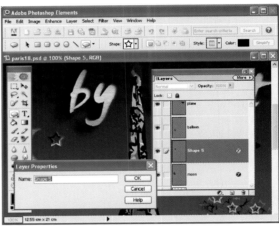

So far we've only added one star but really we want the whole sky to be full of them. We could do this by creating new shape layers for each star but this would make life unnecessarily complicated. Instead we can add multiple stars to the existing layer by making sure that the second Add to Shape Area mode option is selected on the Custom Shape tool's context-sensitive property bar.

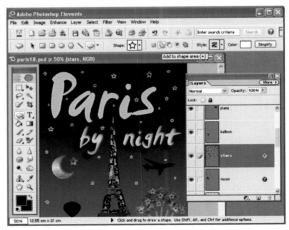

The effect we are looking to create is of more and larger stars towards the darker top of the sky much as occurs in real life. While we're adding the stars we can vary their number and size, but inevitably we'll want to rearrange them and resize them later to produce a more pleasing effect. That's no problem as we can use the Shape Selection tool to pick out individual stars to move, resize and also rotate (very important in this case as it stops them looking too regular).

Now we can fine-tune the overall appearance. We've already applied the Nebula pattern-based layer style which means that the colors vary attractively not only between each star but also within each star. Originally I also planned to add an Outer Glow style to the stars but in practice this was too fussy and distracting so instead let's add the Simple glow style to the moon's shape layer and call up the Style Settings dialog to fine-tune its size.

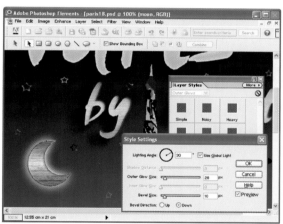

Applying the finishing touches

We're very nearly there now but, by returning to what we learned earlier about brushes and layer-based compositing, we can add a couple of finishing touches that make a big difference.

To begin with, we can add some more dynamism to the image by adding in the plane's vapour trails. To do this of course we need to add another new layer, select the Brush tool (shortcut B) and then, with the property bar, select a soft round brush and set its size appropriately. Again to mimic the grainy air spray look that we produced for the firework trails we can lower the opacity and set the blending mode to Dissolve. We can then draw two parallel strokes by using the SHIFT key to force the brush to produce straight lines.

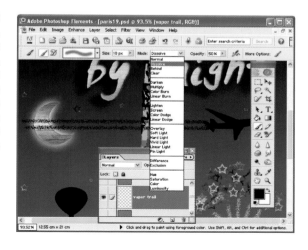

Next using the Move tool (shortcut V) we can rotate the 'Vapour Trails' layer to give them a slight upward angle which we can also pick up in the plane. What we are trying to do is to underscore the title with a flourish – the message is clear and positive: onward and upward.

It's a positive message but it's also meant to be subtle and subliminal and, as it stands, the vapour trail is the most eye-catching element in the whole image. That's easily remedied though, first of all by using the Eraser tool (shortcut E) to rub out the trails as they cross the tower to move the effect further into the distance. And secondly, by radically lowering the layer's opacity on the Layers palette.

Non-destructive color correction

We've added a lot of dynamism and romanticism to the previously flat sky, but we're in danger of taking attention away from the real focus of attention, namely the Eiffel Tower and Paris, France, itself. We can give these a final boost by using the last of Elements' layer-based features – Adjustment Layers. These work much like the Fill Layer that we used earlier to apply a gradient to the sky but, rather than having a color value themselves, they affect all underlying pixel values.

Before we apply the Adjustment Layer we need to ensure that only the tower and foreground of the image are affected. To do this we need to select them and the easiest way to do this is to first select the Sky layer by CTRL/⌘+clicking on it in the Layers palette and then selecting the Select > Inverse command (shortcut CTRL/⌘+SHIFT+I).

Next we need to add the Adjustment Layer using either the first command icon at the bottom of the Layers palette or the Layer > New Adjustment Layer command. There are seven options to choose from and the one we want is Hue/Saturation (shortcut CTRL/⌘+U).

Within the Hue/Saturation dialog we can drag the Saturation slider over to the right to increase the intensity of the colors to make them more vibrant,

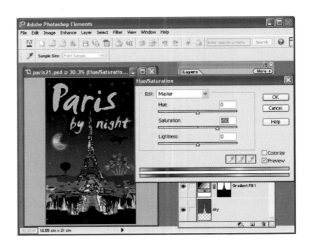

exciting and inviting. We've increased the level dramatically but it's worth pointing out that the version you'll see on screen might well be very different to the printed results as the CMYK (cyan, magenta, yellow and black) inks that most printers depend on aren't capable of producing every color that the RGB (red, green, blue) screen can.

At this stage you might be wondering why we changed the colors using an adjustment layer rather than directly with the Hue/Saturation command available from the Enhance menu. The answer - as always with layers - is flexibility and editability. In particular you can simply double-click on the adjustment layer in the Layers palette to recall its associated dialog and fine-tune your settings. In this case I've slightly increased the lightness of the colors.

And that's it – our image is finished. We've certainly come a long way from our starting image and, if we open the Layers palette, we can look back on how. By combining Photoshop Elements' one-off filters with its handling of image layers, type layers, layer effects, fill layers, shape layers and adjustment layers we've changed our original photograph into a unique work of art.

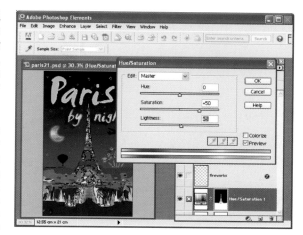

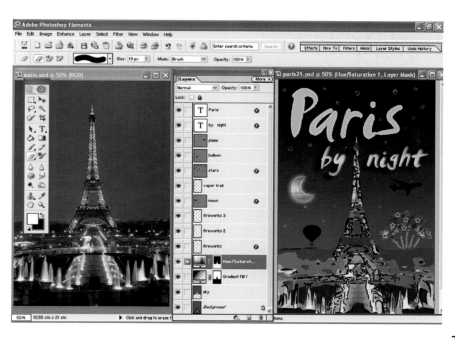

Tom Arah set up his own design company back in 1987 shortly after leaving Edinburgh University. Thanks to the competitive advantage provided by one of the first laser printers and a black-and-white scanner, he built a successful business producing everything from business cards to full-color magazines for everyone from local charities to ruthless multinationals.

Tom still continues his work as a hands-on graphic designer, but has also branched out into training and consultancy where he tries to share the knowledge that he has built up over the years - and tries to stop others making the same mistakes that he did! He has run courses on all of the most popular design packages from Photoshop to Corel Draw and PageMaker to Dreamweaver.

For the last five years, Tom has concentrated on writing about computer-based design. He has worked as a freelance writer for many computer magazines around the world and is now a Contributing Editor for the UK's biggest monthly computer magazine, PC Pro, and for Australia's PC Authority. In this capacity he reviews all the latest PC-based design and graphics software and regularly writes in-depth articles and tutorials. Recently he has turned his hand to writing books.

Other highlights in Tom's portfolio include a prize-winning foray into shareware programming and his role as webmaster for the award-winning designer-info.com site. As well as designing and producing the site, Tom writes all the content, which currently consists of over 200 design software reviews, articles and tutorials - with more added each month. Over one million visitors have visited www.designer-info.com since it went live in 2000.

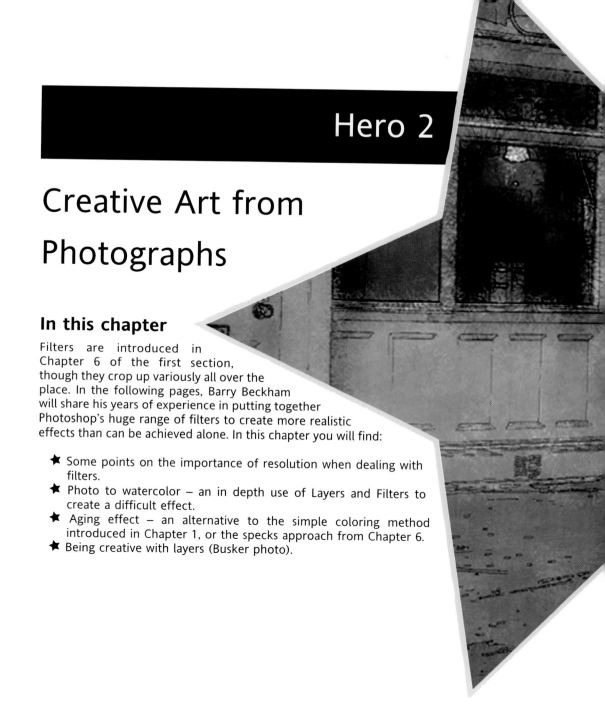

Hero 2

Creative Art from Photographs

In this chapter

Filters are introduced in Chapter 6 of the first section, though they crop up variously all over the place. In the following pages, Barry Beckham will share his years of experience in putting together Photoshop's huge range of filters to create more realistic effects than can be achieved alone. In this chapter you will find:

★ Some points on the importance of resolution when dealing with filters.

★ Photo to watercolor – an in depth use of Layers and Filters to create a difficult effect.

★ Aging effect – an alternative to the simple coloring method introduced in Chapter 1, or the specks approach from Chapter 6.

★ Being creative with layers (Busker photo).

★ Hero

Modern image editing software is bags of fun for all sorts of reasons and Photoshop Elements is definitely not short in the fun department. In fact Elements 2 has sacks full of fun and when we apply one of the many filters that come with the software, it can be almost magical as we turn a photograph into a work of art!

However, adding filter effects to images often gets the thumbs down. This is because filter effects are easy to apply and often get used on the wrong image to cover up a multitude of sins. They can also be applied quickly and easily and this encourages repeated use. Turkey for Christmas is nice, but if we had it every weekend, it wouldn't be long before we were bored stiff with it! To work well, filter effects need to be used sparingly and on the right choice of picture.

The first thing to remember with all filter effects is that the effect of the filter will be greater on lower resolution images. For example: A filter effect applied to a 2 MB file may look quite nice, but the same settings applied to an 18 MB probably won't. It is all down to the resolution, but let's not become too bogged down with that just yet.

If you don't get the result you are looking for first time, reduce the resolution of your image and have another go. These filters work by adjusting the pixels within our images. As the resolution of modern cameras has increased, the effect of the filter is less noticeable. That may be an advantage with some images where the filter effect is more delicate. The best way to evaluate the effect you have applied is to view your image at the print size. Within Elements you can do that by selecting the Zoom tool and clicking the print size button from the Options bar.

If the filter effect does not look attractive, reduce the resolution and try the filter again. In some respects filters do degrade the image, but in a controlled way that leads to a specific effect. It's fine in these circumstances to reduce the resolution, but always retain an original at full resolution.

To really get people's attention, the trick is to do something that others aren't doing so that your filter effect cannot be obtained by a click of a button.

Reducing resolution

Our two example images of this male ape are exactly the same size, both being 14" x 11", but the difference between them is the resolution. The top image has a resolution of 180 pixels per square inch and weighs in at 15 MB while the lower image is only at 72 ppi resolution and weighs in at just 2.4 MB. On screen, at print size we won't see any difference between them.

In the Filter menu of Elements you will find the Artistic set of filters and among them there's one called Dry Brush.... If we apply that filter to both our images we can see a considerable difference in the effect. In this example we'll use the default options of the filter, as can be seen in the screenshot.

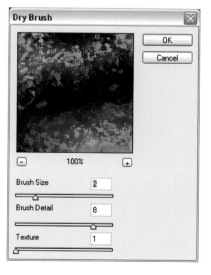

The lower resolution image shows a marked difference and at the print size of 14" x 11" the filter effect can clearly be seen. This filter paints an image using an effect that is something like an oil painting or a watercolor. The filter simplifies the image by reducing its range of colors to areas of common color.

This filter has been chosen to show the differences we can expect to see between high and low resolution images using some filter effects. The Dry Brush filter shows the difference particularly well. Don't forget to view your work at the print size before finally making a decision on the application of that particular filter.

However, the higher resolution image doesn't show the effect nearly so well. The higher resolution has not given us a very nice effect and in fact it has made the image look poor quality rather than filtered.

To reduce the resolution of an image select Image > Resize > Image size… from the Menu bar. Photoshop presents us with the Image Size palette and it's from here that we can reduce the resolution. The screenshot to the right shows the settings for our image.

If we highlight the Resolution box and type in a new resolution of 72, Photoshop will increase the width and height of our image considerably, although the size remains at 15 MB, which is not what we wish to do.

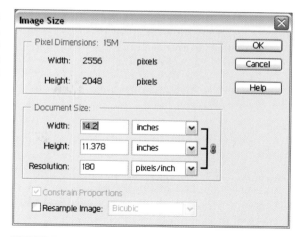

If we check the Resample Image box and reduce the resolution to 72 again, there is a different result. Rather than increasing the actual size as before, Photoshop has kept our image at 14" x11" by removing pixels, which also reduces the file size to about 2.4 MB.

How much of the resolution we finally decide to remove to get the particular filter effect we want will depend to some extent on the content of the image. For example, is the image "fussy" with lots of detail or is it a big bold subject. A subject with lots of detail will need a greater resolution, so that not too much of it will be lost in the filter process.

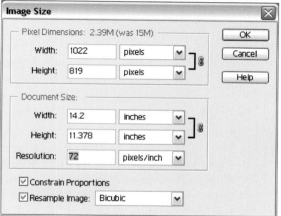

An image will generally look different on screen than it will in print, which is why we always need to view the filtered image at print size. It's difficult to be specific and say how much resolution we should take out to get the filter effect we want, but 72 dpi is about the lowest we should go.

Photo to watercolor

Our image was shot with a Nikon Coolpix 990 camera and it came up on screen straight from the camera at 9 MB in size. The image has some appeal and the wet day will lend itself well to a watercolor effect.

We will be using a filter effect to change our image, but often our chosen filter can have too great an effect on our image if used on its own.

★ Hero

To counteract that we can use another layer and another effect that will create edge lines around the subject matter. This will hold our shape detail, while the filter effect creates the charm.

We can then blend the two layers and make final adjustments here and there.

Step 1: Cropping, cloning, and levels

Before applying any filter techniques it's always good practice to make some standard initial adjustments to an image first. In our example we've used the Crop tool to remove a little of the white edge on the left hand side of the picture.

Wherever possible, we should avoid having light areas on the edges of our pictures. Light parts of an image draw the viewer's eye and we don't want to direct their attention to the edge of our image.

There is a small piece of a white window up in the top right of the image and we can deal with that using the Clone tool.

The Clone tool is best used with the image greatly enlarged, perhaps up to something like 300%. Hold down the ALT key and sample an area close to what you need to cover. Release the ALT key, and using a soft edged brush click down over the offending area, in our case, the white window frame.

We should always check out the color levels as well at this stage. Click Enhance > Adjust Brightness/Contrast and adjust the levels. This subject has been covered in Chapter 1 and normally we would try and stay away from "auto" buttons. However, we are going to make significant changes in our image via filter effects anyway and in this case the Auto Levels command via Enhance > Autolevels works fine. After doing these initial changes this is a good point to save the project, in case we want to come back to this point later.

We are almost certainly going to have to do a little work at the top of our image with the lighter tones recorded there. We will be using Copy and Paste via a selection, to copy darker pixels and transfer them over unwanted lighter areas.

Step 2: Duplicate layer

To start the filter process we need to make a layer copy and we can do that in a couple of ways. From the Docking Well at the top right of the screen we need to select the Layers tab.

From the Layers palette, we then click and drag the thumbnail of our image down over the Copy icon, and Photoshop creates a duplicate layer for us.

Alternatively, we can select Layer > Duplicate layer from the menu at the top of the screen and this creates another layer in the same way, but also gives us the opportunity to name it.

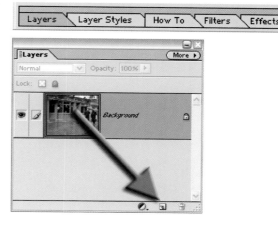

We can rename a layer from within the Layers palette at any time by right-clicking the thumbnail and choosing Rename Layer....

Step 3: Smart Blur and Soft Light

First, we will create our lined effect on the upper layer and to do this we will be using the Smart Blur filter, from the Filter menu. Select Filter > Blur > Smart Blur..., and Elements will bring up the options for this filter. For our image, we are going to set the Quality option to High and the Mode option to Edge Only. The Radius and Threshold sliders enable us to create more or less lines, but for our image we'll leave them at the default setting. When we click OK, Photoshop will recreate our image as white lines on a black background.

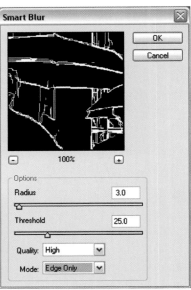

We actually need black lines on a white background so that when we blend our lined layer with our layer at the bottom of the stack, the blend process creates the effect we are looking for. This is simply achieved via Image > Adjustments > Invert or via the shortcut keys of CTRL/⌘+I.

From the drop-down in the Layers tab, select Soft Light. As the lined layer is blended with the original layer, we can already see how the image is beginning to take on a watercolor type effect. Now we've got this far, it's a good idea to save the project again. We need to save the image as a PSD to ensure that the layers are saved as well.

Step 4: Filter

We can now apply the filter effect we want to the bottom layer. From within the Layers tab, click on the original layer at the bottom of the stack.

The choices of filter effect we can run on this image can be wide and various and a quick look through the filters shows that there are many to choose from. With this type of work it is not always possible to predict what filter will give an attractive result and which one will not. It is down to a little trial and error, but that's half the fun of digital imaging.

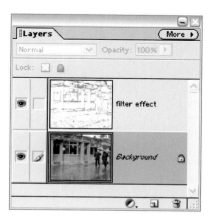

It's a good idea to try a series of different artistic filters on our images and save each one. It can be fun to compare the results later and while we are doing that our knowledge and experience is increasing.

At this stage, we can experiment with the many artistic filters that come with Elements or even those third party filters that we can add later.

For our choice of filter for this project, we'll stay within the artistic filter pack. We need to look for filters such as Dry Brush, Paint Daubs, Palette Knife, Underpainting, and Watercolor, but experimentation is the key. These filters will affect the pixels on this bottom layer much like we saw with the Dry Brush filter earlier, but the lined layer will retain the shapes we want.

The resulting image is beginning to come together, but needs more work to complete the process. You may notice that the layer blend process has caused the tones to be a little weak. This is simply due to our lined layer being predominantly white, but we can fix that fairly easily with our levels command.

Step 5: Re-adjusting tones

Before we adjust the tone levels, we need to combine the two layers we created. Before doing this it's a good idea to save another copy of the image. To flatten the layers, simply select Layer > Flatten Image.

Once both layers are combined we can then adjust those levels. The Levels palette is opened by clicking Enhance > Adjust Brightness/Contrast > Levels…, or using the shortcut keys Ctrl/⌘+L.

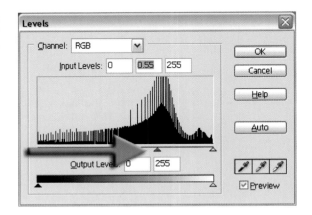

In this image we need to move the center slider that controls the image midtones to the right. The effect is a darkening of the midtones and as we move the slider to the right we see the impact to our image increase before our eyes.

If we examine the image critically, we can see what still needs to be done.

The top of the image is a little too bright along the top edge and the bottom of the pavement could also take some further adjustment to darken the tones still further. Remember that lighter tones attract the eye and we need to avoid them falling on the edge of our picture area if we can. Darkening the pavement and dealing with those light areas at the top of the image will concentrate the viewer's attention within the picture, just where we want it.

Let's deal with the pavement first, but before we move on, this is another good point at which to save the image again.

Step 6: Selections

We need to adjust the tone levels for the pavement area, but not in the rest of the image, so we can do this by making a selection. Using the Lasso tool we can draw around the pavement area. Before we make any adjustments, we need to add a degree of feather to the selection line. This will soften the edge and make our manipulations blend nicely into the image.

We add feathering by clicking Select > Feather… and selecting a radius in pixels. For our image we will choose 150 pixels. The choice of feather radius for any given effect can be a personal one depending on personal tastes. However, in an image where we want to affect pixels without our manipulations being seen, a higher value will be necessary. The feather radius is affected by the resolution of our image in the same way as our filters.

★ Hero

So for high resolution pictures a higher feather value may be required. In our case here, the actual radius is not too critical and anything over 100 would give an effect we could live with.

Before selecting the Levels palette again, it's helpful if we hide the selection line as it allows us to judge the work better. Pressing CTRL/⌘+H hides the line, but the selection remains active along with the feathered edge. Hitting CTRL/⌘+H again reveals the selection.

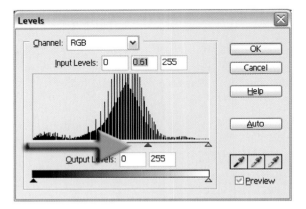

If we reopen the Levels palette, we can move the center slider towards the right as we did before, but this time just darkening the pavement area. When that's done, pressing CTRL/⌘+D removes the lasso selection.

The more solid tones introduced at the bottom of the image now make our image far stronger and we are now ready to turn our attention to the top. Once again, we are at a good point to save another copy of the image.

Step 7: Copy and Paste patching

Turning our attention to those light tones at the top of the image we need to find a way of darkening them or removing them. One of the options we could consider is cropping from the top, but while that may be better than doing nothing, it would take something away from the appeal of the picture. We can do better than that by using the Copy and Paste options along with the Layers palette. We can copy those darker pixels and then use them as a patch, covering the unwanted lighter tones along the top of the picture.

This patch technique can be used in many images where tones have been lost. It is a good alternative to the Clone Stamp tool where its use may be difficult or the area fairly large. It involves us making a selection of those good pixels and applying that good old feather radius again. We can then copy our patch with our feathered edge to a new layer. Our copied pixels can then be dragged over the light tones in the form of a patch.

We need to start by using the Zoom tool to enlarge the top right of the image to about 200%. At this size we can see and use our selection tools far more accurately. Then we can use the Lasso tool to make a selection of the good tones just above the blue-fronted bar.

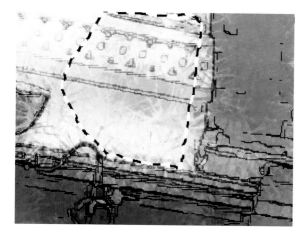

Using that Feather palette again we can add a 5 pixel feather radius to the selection. If we then select Edit > Copy and then Edit > Paste from the Menu bar, Photoshop will copy just the selection to a new layer. If we then open the Layers palette we will see the layer we've created, called Layer 1 in the screenshot to the right. Hitting the tiny eye on the bottom layer makes it invisible, so we can just see the copied selection. This layer is what we are going to use as a patch to cover the light areas.

To do this, we need to click the eye again so that the bottom layer is visible, and then select the Move tool from the top right of the Toolbar. We can then drag our patch to cover up the white area. We needn't worry about covering the floodlights that caused the highlights; they're not essential to our image.

As we did earlier, we can make another copy of the patch by dragging the thumbnail over the Copy icon. We can then move that patch along to cover the next light area, and repeat this process along the entire shop front. Depending on the number of patches we need, the Layers tab will get quite full, so once all the patching is completed, we can select Layer > Flatten Image and merge all those layers into one. We need to remember to save the image first though!

Step 8: The Burn tool

Now that the highlights have been removed from the shop front, the next things to consider tweaking are the bright white window frame and shopping bag. To darken these we can use the Burn tool. From the Range options that appear at the top of the screen, we need to select Highlights, and for Exposure, a setting of 5% is adequate. We can now use the mouse to gently darken the window frame and the shopping bag.

Looking at the original photo again for comparison, it's easy to see what a difference we've made. The original glossy photo has been easily transformed into a convincing impressionist watercolor. As you can see there are lots of little steps to adding a convincing filter effect, but they are well worth the effort and by using several steps *carefully*, we will end up with something unique and exciting.

You may be wondering why we saved the image at so many stages, and the answer is this: for insurance. It's inevitable as we strive to create ever more new and worthy looks that we're going to come across far more bad ones. When experimenting, we're never entirely sure if our manipulations will work out well, and if they don't, then having the project saved at various stages means we can go back and try something else. It's all part of the digital rollercoaster!

Textures

Filter effects can often be enhanced further by the addition of a texture effect. Although our watercolor image from the last section looks fine, let's see how we can take it a little further with a texture filter. These textures can look delightful when printed as long as they're not overdone. Let's see how.

First, we select Filter > Texture > Texturizer... and Photoshop brings up the Texturizer palette. The Texture menu on this palette contains four textures: Brick, Burlap, Canvas, and Sandstone, and also gives us the option to load other textures.

If we select the Load Texture... option, Photoshop opens a window that asks where the textures are. If we follow this path: C:/Applications/Adobe/ Photoshop Elements 2/Presets/Textures, we have a number of other texture choices.

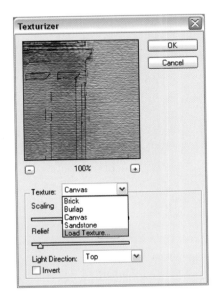

> If you're likely to use these texture filters often, copy this texture folder to a more convenient place on your hard drive.

The Rust Flakes texture (shown right) is a good choice for higher resolution images because the texture shape is bigger and therefore works better on our high resolution image. This is due to the same resolution issue we talked about earlier. If we applied the Rust filter and then the Canvas filter to a high resolution image at the maximum 200% scaling we would see quite a difference. The texture of the Canvas, being so small, may look unattractive and in some cases it can even detract from the image rather than add anything to it. The Rust Flakes texture is a larger texture and therefore shows up better on our higher resolution images.

In the Texturizer palette there is a Scaling setting, as well as a Light Direction, and a Relief slider. The scale chosen will again be affected by the resolution of the image. In our example, which was a high-resolution image, we needed to select the maximum of 200% to achieve a pleasing result. The relief (or depth of the texture) for the delicate texture we have applied here was a setting of 4, but this option is also one where personal preference comes in.

We can try the Burlap texture (shown right), which also works well with higher resolution images. However, running the Canvas texture on high resolution images at small sizes does not give a good effect. Try it!

Frames

Images can also be enhanced with a frame and there are a number of ready-made frames within Photoshop Elements 2 that can be applied, so let's explore one or two of those and apply them to our now textured watercolor.

If we click the Effects tab in the Docking Well and then select Frames from the drop-down menu, we are presented with a number of ready-made choices.

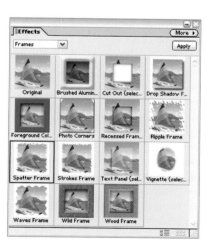

★ Hero

The Brushed Aluminum frame automatically adds some depth via a drop shadow. We just need to double-click the option and Photoshop applies it to our image. Try out the other choices too.

If you're feeling a bit more ambitious, you can try the following steps for a more unique frame.

Step 1: Stroke command

First, we click the Layers tab from the Docking Well and double-click the image thumbnail and in the New Layer box type a new name. Any name will do, but in our case Watercolor seems appropriate.

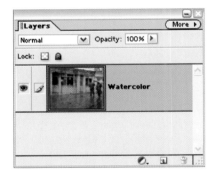

Using the keyboard shortcut of CTRL/⌘+A, we can select the outer edge of the image.

From the Menu bar we then select Edit > Stroke...
and Photoshop will open the Stroke options
palette. Let's choose white as the Color option and
for the Location option select Inside, with a pixel
width of 3-6 pixels, and click OK, Photoshop will
then apply a thin white line to the edge of our
picture.

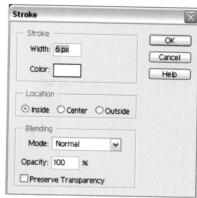

Step 2: Canvas size

Now we want to select Image > Resize > Canvas
Size... and add a couple of inches to the height
and width. The new canvas is shown as gray and
white checks.

If we select the Layers tab from the Docking Well
and click the center one of the three icons at the
bottom right, Photoshop will create a new blank
layer. We then need to click on the blank layer
thumbnail and drag it below the Watercolor layer.

This new blank layer is where we will create our
border, so it needs to be beneath the Watercolor
layer. When we apply color to that layer, that color
will show through from beneath all around the
edges.

Step 3: Color sampling and cloud effect

The next thing to do is to select the Eyedropper tool from the Toolbar. We can click anywhere on the picture and the color we clicked appears as the foreground color in the Color Picker. Holding the ALT key while using the Eyedropper lets us sample a background color. We need to sample two colors from within our picture.

We chose two of the darker colors from our picture because we do not want to introduce light tones to our border. The actual choice of the two colors is again a personal one, and some trial and error is needed. You will not always make the right choices first time, but as we said earlier, it's all part of the fun.

Select Filter > Render > Clouds, and Photoshop will create a cloud structure using the two colors we sampled and flood that onto our new blank layer.

Step 4: Hue and saturation

To make our frame just right, we need to reduce the color saturation and the lightness of our clouds a little. We can do this via the Hue/Saturation palette. We can open this palette by clicking Enhance > Adjust Color > Hue/Saturation... or use the shortcut keys of CTRL/⌘+U.

How much we darken the clouds depends on the image we're working on. If it looks right to you, then it probably is. With some images where the tones within the image are much lighter, we may even decide to lighten the border a little.

Step 5: Adding Noise

The final touch for our frame is to add a few pixels of Noise, just to add a little texture to it. When we add computer-generated color to any photographic image it can look rather plastic when printed. This is because in comparison to the photographic image the computer generated color looks too smooth, maybe not on the screen, but certainly on a print.

We can put that right using the Noise filter and in the case of our border we can increase the effect a little to produce a nice texture. Clicking Filters > Noise > Add Noise… opens the Add Noise panel where we can choose to add between 0.1 and 400% Noise. If the Preview box is checked, we can see the border change as we move the slider. For this example about 3-4% gives the right effect.

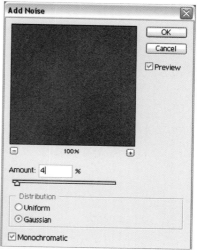

Aging effect

Here we have an image that has that olde-worlde feel to it, but perhaps we can add to that aged look with another of Photoshop Elements filters, the Craquelure effect, which we can apply by selecting Filter > Texture > Craquelure….

The image in this example is 10 inches by 7.5 inches at 200 dpi.

When the Craquelure options palette pops onto the screen we can see from the preview screen that the default settings are far too harsh for even this high resolution image. It breaks up the face of our soldier so much that it does little to enhance our work.

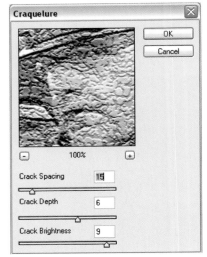

If we increase the Crack Spacing with the slider control and keep an eye on the preview panel we can produce a far better result. How much spacing you introduce is a personal choice, but for our image 60 is about right.

The Crack Depth and Crack Brightness settings also depend on personal choice, but they don't have quite the marked effect on the filter like the Crack Spacing slider.

This is another one of those examples where a reduction in resolution may help to create a better effect. If we click Image > Resize > Image Size... we can decrease the resolution from 200 ppi down to 100 ppi.

Make sure the Resample Image box is ticked so that when we drop the 200 dpi to 100 the size in inches remains the same.

The effect now using the same settings is better and we have given our image an aged look.

Let's take this just a little bit further with a sepia tone. If we select Enhance > Adjust Color > Hue/Saturation... and tick the Colorize box on the palette that appears, this is the result we get.

Here we can adjust the Hue slider and balance that with the Saturation slider to give a sepia tone to our image. These sliders give us lots of control to produce just the right depth of sepia tone we want.

Busker

Here we are going to use a number of layers to produce a unique effect. This process of blending four layer effects together was freely passed onto me by a good friend of mine, Barry Colquhoun, who was the person who encouraged me to start writing tutorials in the first instance. Thanks mate!

One of the four layers is there for insurance, just in case we need to use some of that layer later. Often these filter effects can destroy some detail that we actually want and that insurance layer may be useful.

On another layer we will create our filter effects and then use another to put back color lost in that filter process. Finally we will blend our filter effect with one of our original layers using the Opacity command in the Layers palette.

For this example we are going to use an image of a busker, taken on the streets of Melbourne, Australia.

Step 1: Plastic Wrap

The first thing we need to do is to make those three extra layer copies of our image, which we can do in the Layers palette as we saw earlier.

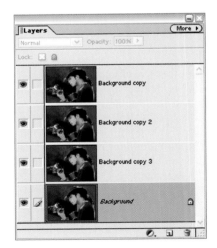

Now we need to select our original layer from the bottom of the stack and click Filter > Artistic > Plastic Wrap.... The sliders in the Plastic Wrap panel allow us some control, but we can try using the default settings first. Don't forget to click the little eye of all the layers above the one we are working on, so we can see the effects of our work. We need to temporarily turn those layers off.

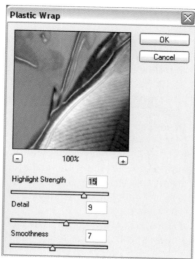

Step 2: Cutout filter

Again from the Artistic filters we now select the Cutout... filter and apply it to the same layer as the plastic wrap. We've used the default settings again for this filter, although there is plenty of scope for experimentation with different settings. The effect doesn't look much at the moment, but it will get better.

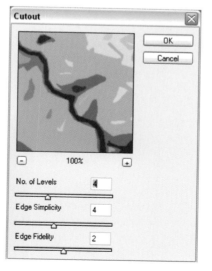

Step 3: Merge layers

Now we select the second layer, one up from the bottom of the layers stack. As we click on the thumbnail, the layer will become live and ready for editing and the eye will automatically reveal the layer. From the drop-down menu at the top left of the Layers tab we choose Color. This will put back the color that we have lost in the filter process so far.

At this point we should save the work and merge the bottom two layers together. To do this we uncheck the little eye icon in the top two layers in the Layers tab, and then select Layers > Merge Visible from the Menu Bar. Photoshop will merge those two filtered layers into one, leaving three layers.

Step 4: Opacity

Carrying on, we select the middle of the three layers and using the Opacity slider in the Layers tab, reduce the opacity of this layer until we have a little of each showing. We found that about 30% opacity was about right and just brings back a little of the original.

With the top layer turned off we can now merge those bottom two layers.

Step 5: Eraser

The layer at the top of the layer stack is our insurance. Often, when we apply filter effects to faces more detail is lost than we would like. Keeping that layer gives us the opportunity to repair that detail.

To do that we need to rename our filtered layer, so we can drag the unfiltered layer down to the bottom of the stack.

With the filtered layer as the top layer, we can select it again and use the Eraser tool to 'rub through' it in places to reveal a little of the unfiltered layer beneath.

Step 6: Final tweaks

We can now finish off the image with final adjustments to the color and contrast, as well as doing any cloning that may be needed.

Once we have completed our work we need to flatten any remaining layers and the command to flatten layers together is found via Layer > Flatten image. This type of image can also be enhanced still further, by applying a texture effect as we described earlier.

As we said at the start of this section, adding filters often gets the thumbs down. This is by those who want their art at a click of a button, but one-click effects get boring.

We hope we've shown here just what fun it is mixing filter effects together with a few other tips and tricks to make your images special. We've not found all the secrets of Photoshop Elements 2 yet, and somewhere inside the software there are many more. It just needs you to set out on your own journey to discover them, remember that experimentation is the key and what makes digital imaging so much fun. Don't settle for the same filter effects as everyone else, do something different!

As we apply different filter effects there are almost always some downsides to doing so. We have talked earlier about how faces for example can look odd after a filter is applied. We need to look critically at each stage and be prepared to repair the parts that have gone wrong. Nothing worthwhile is created in two minutes, spend some time, some thought and be patient. Mix those attributes with a little creativity and you are away on the journey.

★ Hero

The author of our filter effect section is Barry Beckham. Barry is 53 years old and lives in the eastern suburbs of London, UK. He has been interested in photography as a hobby for over 25 years and in the early days he joined a local Camera Club to learn the craft. Barry quickly became involved in all the club activities, which are wide and various. He learned how to develop and print his own black and white images and took part in competitions and exhibitions with his images.

Barry discovered Adobe Photoshop some years ago, in its early days, and digital imaging grabbed him in a big way. He says that he now realizes he was a digital photographer all his life, just waiting for the technology to be invented.

Barry was captivated by the creativity Photoshop allowed even in its early days, but the price of that software is a little prohibitive for many amateurs. What makes Photoshop Elements 2 so good is that we now have almost all the power of Adobe Photoshop at a fraction of the cost. In addition Photoshop Elements 2 has been put together with amateur digital photographers in mind. The tools and processes have been designed for ease of use and the help menus are much improved. There is little excuse now for anyone who wishes to either improve their digital photographs or create completely new ones. Barry now works "100% digital" using a Nikon Coolpix 990 digital camera and a Canon EOS D60 digital SLR.

Digital photography is not Barry's full-time occupation, but that does not mean he is not dedicated and professional in the work he produces. He writes regularly for the UK digital magazines and has written for Digital Photo since its launch. Barry has also written at one time or another for Digital Photography, Digital Photographer, and Digital Photo User.

One of his passions is maintaining his web site and he says that there is nothing like having your own personal picture gallery for the world to see. Barry's web site has grown quite large with almost 50 galleries of images and hundreds of Photoshop tutorials. You can find his site at www.bbdigital.co.uk.

Barry is also kept busy lecturing on Digital Imaging subjects to photographic societies affiliated to the Photographic Alliance of Great Britain. Barry says this is a very rewarding part of his photographic life and he learns almost as much as he teaches in his travels around the clubs and societies.

Fun Family Photography

In this chapter

In this chapter we take a slight break from Photoshop. Don't worry, we're not leaving it behind, but we're going to take a very necessary look at your photography as well as your computer skills. Based on a typical family outing, Paul (not forgetting Jacquie, Jasmine and Eric) share their experience of when, and when not, to resort to Photoshop. All the techniques listed will help you tell a story with your snaps, or at the very least get you thinking:

* ★ Simplifying your photos
* ★ Composition
* ★ Portrait or Landscape
* ★ Avoiding distraction
* ★ Motion blurs
* ★ Telling a story

The typical happy snap

This is Jacquie, Jasmine, and Eric out in the park for the day. This photo is typical of a 'happy snap' and is really a bit of a mess. The main things wrong are:

- ★ The subjects are too far away.
- ★ There are things coming in and out of the edges of the photo all over the place.
- ★ The bags on the seats are not particularly attractive.
- ★ The background is cluttered.
- ★ There is part of a man on the top left edge.
- ★ The right hand side of the photo has nothing exciting in it and is basically empty space.
- ★ No-one is looking at the camera.

Could we have done better?

Yes, changing position to avoid the bags and other people would be a start. Either get closer to subjects or zoom in. Get them to relax by playing a game.

Could we fix it in Elements?

Maybe. Using the Crop tool (Chapter 1) we could remove the empty space and make the people the center of attention.

We would still have to clone out the bags in the background but we cannot do much about the poses. While Elements seems to be magic, you can't effectively fix these sorts of photos. It really is best to get it right when taking the photo.

This is known as composition, which is the technical photographic term for the design of a photo. While this can be a very detailed and obscure subject, even knowing just a few basics will improve your images immensely.

Simplify your photos

Here we have Jasmine on the slide, but this photo would be better described as "Playground equipment, next to a carpark in a forest (child included)". The main things wrong is that the subject is too far away and there are too many things competing for our attention.

The most important part of creating a photo is choosing what to leave out. Keep it simple. Decide what the subject is and have it fill as much of the frame as possible to remove any distractions. The best way to do this is to get in closer. If you only do one thing to improve your photos - do this. If you are taking a photo of someone, it is not mandatory to include their feet!

Could we have done better?

Yes, we need to get closer. Either change position or zoom in. If you are worried about being in people's faces, then use the camera's zoom to get closer while still being at a distance.

Just watch out for vertical and horizontal lines. Here it looks like the play equipment is about to fall over. It is very difficult to both hold the camera exactly level and also to line up the photo straight in the scanner. Do not worry about slight tilts as they can be easily fixed in Elements.

The easiest way to find if your verticals and horizontals are just that is as follows:

1. Ensure that the Info Palette (Chapter Zero) is visible.

2. Select the Line tool (Chapter 5), and set it to 1 pixel width.

3. Draw a line from one end of your object to the other without releasing the mouse button.

4. In the Info palette you will see the angle of the line you have drawn. Here it is 87.9 degrees, which is 2.1 degrees off vertical.

5. Use Undo (Chapter zero) to remove the line you have just drawn.

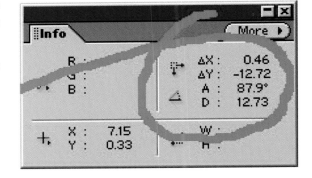

6. Then use Image > Rotate > Custom... to straighten the photo by the amount above.

7. Finally use the Crop tool to remove the extra pixels around the edges.

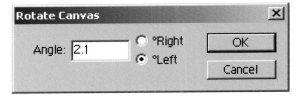

Photo 3: Composition

Here we have Jacquie, Jasmine, and Eric again, but now everyone is more relaxed. While we cannot see the children's faces, it is much better than the first photo because you can feel something of the emotional bond in the group.

When you have a group, try to be in charge. There is nothing more boring than a 'school photo' with everyone lined up. Let people relax, chat or do an activity. But remember that you have the camera, so do not be afraid to politely ask someone to move or look another way. Of course you are not directing a theatre production, so stay low key and relaxed. If you are relaxed your subjects will be too.

There is a photographic compositional rule of thumb that almost always works known as 'The Rule of Thirds' which is as follows.

Imagine placing a grid of lines over your photo in such a way that it is divided into nine even pieces. Your image should be divided along these lines. For a landscape the sky should occupy the top third, then the middle distance, and the foreground in the bottom third. For a seascape the horizon would be on either of the dividing lines. Then you would try to have an item of interest on each of the intersections.

While this is not always possible to do, avoid having things centered in the middle of the photo. Photos can still work with the subject in the center, but they often do not.

Could we have done better?

Yes, the cars and play equipment in the background are a distraction. Changing position to avoid these distractions would have helped.

With an SLR, using a larger aperture size (smaller f number) would have reduced the depth of field which would have blurred the background. Technically this is known as selective depth of field, and it can be rather difficult to predict the exact effect unless your camera has a depth of field preview facility. Depth of field usually is not controllable at all on compact cameras. Don't worry though; the effect can be faked easily in Photoshop Elements.

Could we fix it in Elements?

Simulating a reduced depth of field in principle is not difficult. How easy it is to do will depend on the subject and layout of the photo.

When doing this, remember that objects at different distances from the camera will have different degrees of sharpness, and objects at the same distance will be equally sharp or blurry. Having a flat object going in and out of focus is a dead give away. Often just a touch of blur is all that is needed to deflect the viewer's eye to the subject, which should be sharp.

★ Hero

1. Ensure that the Layers palette is visible.

2. Duplicate the background layer into a new layer (Chapter 2). Call this layer 'Blur'.

3. Apply the Gaussian Blur filter. Set the radius to about 5 pixels. Don't overdo it or the effect will not look realistic.

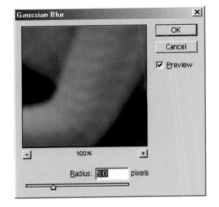

4. In the Layers palette, select the background layer.

5. Create a new Levels Adjustment layer. Just click OK on the dialog box as we will not be making any adjustments, we just need the layer.

6. In the Layers palette select the Blur layer.

7. From the Layers Menu, select the Group with Previous option.

8. In the Layers Palette select the Levels Adjustment layer mask.

9. Select the Gradient tool. Open the Gradient Picker and ensure that it is set to Foreground to Background.

10. Draw a gradient on the image from where you want to be sharp to blurred.

11. Select the Paint Brush tool (Chapter 6) and select a medium sized (20 pixels) soft brush set to 20% opacity.

12. Paint in black on the Levels layer mask anything you want to be sharper. Paint in white anything that you want less sharp. If you make a mistake just undo or paint over it in the other color.

The finished results should look like this.

Format

The shape of the standard photo taken by most cameras is rectangular, with one side being about one and a half times the size of the other. It is important that you remember that you can hold your camera either with the long side horizontally or vertically. These are often known as Landscape or Portrait but do not let the names fool you. Use horizontal for anything that is wider than it is tall (such as a landscape or a person lying down). Use vertical for anything that is taller than it is wide (such as an office tower or a person standing up). Changing the format can have a dramatic effect on your photo.

Could we have done better?

Yes, this photo would be better suited to a vertical format as all of the trees on the sides are just wasted space and changing our point of view would eliminate the parked cars in the background.

You have knees - use them. Do not be afraid to squat, lie down or move around. Look at your subject from as many different positions as possible before taking the photo.

Here is an exercise. Find a single subject, such as a statue or small tree. Take as many different

photos of just this one subject as possible. Using a whole roll of film (or digital memory card – you can always wipe them) on this one subject would be excellent. Remember this exercise before you take every photo.

Could we fix it in Elements?

By using the Crop tool we could eliminate the distracting cars and the empty space. In case you are wondering - yes, I do use the Crop tool a lot. It is the best and easiest way of removing distracting objects. It is even better if you do this with the camera before taking the photo.

This photo is a little dark so use the Enhance > Fill Flash... lighting effect (Chapter 1) to brighten it, or a manual Levels adjustment. The result is a little grainy due to the loss of resolution from all of the pixels that were thrown away when we cropped the photo but it is still usable.

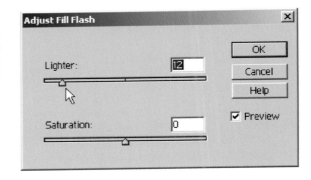

Distracting objects

A distracting object is anything that draws the viewers eye away from the subject. In this photo Eric appears to have a light pole growing out of his head. It is best to avoid this sort of merger between your subject and distracting objects.

Could we have done better?

We might have been able to change position, but if we wanted a head on view there is not much we can do about this background. Using a wider aperture (smaller f number) on an SLR would have blurred the background, but the pole might still have been visible and we would have lost the detail of the forest.

Could we fix it in Elements?

Yes! This is the sort of thing where Elements shines. If you use a traditional darkroom, removing things like this is very difficult, but with Elements it only takes a few moments with the Clone Stamp tool.

Some tips on cloning:

★ Start by creating a new layer then setting the Use All Layers option on the Clone Stamp tool. This makes it easy to correct any errors as you can go back to the original at any time.

★ Set the opacity of the Clone Stamp tool to 50% and use a medium sized (20 pixel) soft brush. Always use a soft brush to help blend the cloned area into its new surroundings.

★ Make a series of dabs on small sections of the object at a time, resampling from different nearby areas often. This helps to make the result look similar to the surrounding areas but also different. By doing this you are far less likely to get the repeated pattern effects that sometimes happens when cloning.

★ Make sure that any shadows cast by the object are removed as well.

Cloning is also useful for removing the various dust, scratches, and hairs that are often found when scanning photos. Simply zoom in closely, and scroll left to right, up, and down until you've covered the whole image.

Elements does include a Dust & Scratches filter, but you should only use it once you have selected the damaged area. It is not meant to be applied to the whole photo. I have not had much success with it as I do not like the effect it gives.

Lighting

Technically, when you photograph an object it is not the object that you capture but the light reflected from it. Without any light everything would be black and photography would not be possible.

It is often suggested that when outdoors the sun should be over your shoulder. This is not good advice. While there is plenty of light in this position, often it causes the subjects to squint, which is not a good look! Instead try to place your subjects in a lightly shaded area out of direct sunlight.

Do not be afraid to have the sun behind the subjects, as in this photo. This is known as backlighting or *contre-jour* lighting. Notice how the sunlight has caught their hair so that it glows, which can be particularly attractive. To do this successfully you will need to use a flash.

If you have ever watched a professional photographer at work you may have wondered why they were using a flash outside in the daylight. This is not because they did not know how to turn it off - they do know what they are doing. Using flash with daylight is known as fill-in flash and helps to reduce the shadows caused by the position of the sun. Most cameras will have to have the flash manually set in these conditions, as it will not activate automatically. Refer to your instruction manual.

Remember that the typical flash in your camera has a range of two to three meters (six to nine feet). To avoid disappointment do not be like the people who try to flash the stage from the balcony at concerts. It just will not reach that far. Only use a flash if the subject is in range.

Motion

The speed of the camera shutter is able to freeze the movement of all but the fastest subjects. While this can be useful, often part of the emotional appeal of a photo is to be able to see the movement as this makes it more dynamic. If you freeze all movement, what is the difference between a sports car hurtling along at full speed and one parked stationary on the track?

To be able to show movement successfully you need to follow the movement of the subject with the camera. The result should be that the subject is sharp and the background is a blurred streak. Technically this is known as panning and while it is not hard to do the results can be unpredictable.

The technique is as follows.

- ★ If possible set the camera to a slow shutter speed. Try about 1/60 of a second to start with, you can experiment with even slower speeds when you have the technique right.
- ★ If the subject will be in range activate your flash.
- ★ Hold your camera firmly and follow the movement of the subject with an even motion from the waist.
- ★ Have a few practice pans before taking the photo.
- ★ Just before the subject is directly in front of you, release the shutter.
- ★ Do not stop the camera. Follow through with the subjects travel.
- ★ Take several photos as most will not work out.

Could we have done better?

This photo is an example of what happens when you do not use panning. The child is blurred and the background is sharp and it just does not look right. Using a faster shutter speed would have frozen the movement but then we would have had a very stationary photo when obviously there should be movement and it still would not have looked right.

Panning with a slow shutter speed allows a photo to show the movement of the subject.

★ Hero

Could we fix it in Elements?

Normally this photo would be destined for the bin, but we can make it usable with the help of the Motion Blur filter.

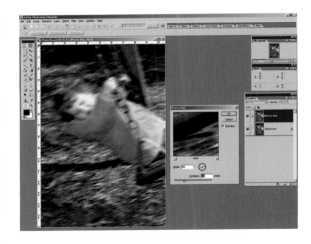

1. Ensure that the Layers palette is visible.

2. Duplicate the background layer into a new layer (Chapter 2). Call this layer 'Motion Blur'.

3. Apply the Motion Blur filter. Set the radius to about 50 pixels. Do not overdo it or the effect will not look realistic. Make sure that the angle of the blur matches the direction of travel of the subject.

4. In the Layers palette select the background layer.

5. Create a new Levels Adjustment layer. Just click OK on the dialog box as we will not be making any adjustments, we just need the layer.

6. In the Layers palette select the Motion Blur layer.

7. From the Layers Menu pull down select the Group with Previous option.

8. In the Layers palette select the Levels Adjustment layer mask.

9. Select the Paint Brush tool (Chapter 6) and using a medium sized (20 pixels) soft brush set to 20% opacity, paint in black on the Levels layer mask anything you want to be sharper. Paint in white anything that you want less sharp. If you make a mistake, just undo or paint over it in the other color.

10. You do not have to be too precise with your painting as these photos are often quite blurry anyway.

11. Make sure that the subjects' eyes are the sharpest point of the photo, even if this means blurring some sharp areas.

The finished results should look something like this.

Tell a Story

Most people do not take enough photos. By this I do not mean taking photos more often, though the film manufactures would certainly like that. If an occasion is worth taking one photo then it deserves many.

I am sure that this experience would have happened to most people. You take a photo of something special and when you pick up the prints from being processed you find that that it did not come out. What a disappointment. It is this result that makes people give up on photography and put their cameras away in the bottom draw – the wrong response. The problem is that there are so many things that can go wrong when you take a photo, that you really need to take several photos to get one good one.

If you consider all the costs of going on a holiday, such as transport, accommodation, expenses, time, then really film is the cheapest part of photography. If it is a special occasion then it is not going to happen again if the photo doesn't work out.

If you are using a digital camera, then you really don't have any excuse at all. Take lots of photos.

If you have several photos of the one subject then you can combine them to tell a story. Here is Jasmine on a swing. She is not sure about this to start off with, but once she finds her mummy we get a pretty smile.

On this photo shoot I took 36 photos in one hour. I would have liked to have taken more but Eric and Jasmine wanted to go on the bouncy castle where I wasn't allowed to take my camera. After an hour they were tired and needed to go home for a nap.

The moral of the story is that you cannot always control the situation. If you do not take the photo when you have the opportunity, you might not get a second chance. One not quite right photo is better than no photo at all. If you get a second chance then you will have two photos to choose from.

Remember to have fun and take lots of photos. Don't worry if some don't work out, many others will. Professional photographers may only get one good photo on a roll, they just do not have to show us the ones that don't work out. Neither do you.

Remember to have fun, get closer and take lots of photos.

Hero 4

Surreal Special Effects

In this chapter

Todd, a professional photographer, shows us seamless use of layers to create an unusual image (and one you definitely wouldn't want to have to create without the aid of digital magic). This is the most advanced chapter in the book, but if you're having trouble, more about layers can be found in Chapter 3. This chapter will take all the below further:

★ Finding concepts
★ The shoot
★ Blending modes
★ Burning shadows

Finding a concept

This image was developed for a self-promotion piece that gets mailed out to about 500 prospects and clients. Concepts like this are the conclusion of looking through magazines, other publications, viewing creative commercials or other advertising to generate some ideas. The concept has to be amusing, involving kids and be plausible. The viewer needs to look at the photo and try to think, was that possible or was it put together? The general public is much more savvy than in years past. They know typically if something has been imaged on a computer. So it becomes more of a challenge to build an image that didn't look like there was a computer involved. But with that said, even images that have obvious signs of manipulation can sometimes be successful.

The fish shot seemed to work in the concept stage because it's funny. It's something a girl this age might try, and it gets you to look and ask how was it done? Is it real? Was it shot in a huge fish tank? And depending on who you are and what your interests are, you may just be amused enough to flick onto the next page or photo. It's an attention grabber. Or if you're like me, you'd pick it apart and try to figure out how they did that. So, let me show you exactly how it was done...

The photography

Once the concept is drawn up with a pencil sketch, it is passed around several colleagues, including my wife who is a graphic designer. If those people get it and are amused or intrigued, the idea moves onto the most important stage... the "how the heck can I pull this off" stage?

This shot had 2 main images and 6-8 detail shots all assembled in post-production using Photoshop only. The catch basin was constructed out of 2 x 6's screwed together to form a 12 x 8 form on the floor in the studio.

The basin had a thick plastic liner to catch the water from the hose. It was held in place by spring clamps. The liner was double layered for extra strength and in case the first layer sprang a leak.

One of the tricky parts was to keep the furniture from getting too wet so the cabinet was placed on the outside of the basin. This was the top half of the shot. The bottom half and the hard part was to remove the catch basin, place the floor down and put the furniture back in exactly the same spot. This whole time the camera was securely anchored on a mono stand so it wouldn't move. The 2 shots need to be made with precision and with exactly the same light so they could be seamed together.

That was another reason the cabinet was placed outside the basin. It has to stay in the same spot and would have been too difficult to move and get the props back in exactly the same spot.

The second shot is taken with the catch basin removed and the floor in place. Then this shot was photographed through a 50-gallon fish tank. The purpose of the fish tank was twofold; to add some distortion and color shift to the part of the shot that was to be underwater and secondly to make a distorted water line that I could strip into the layered file.

Another image I needed to shoot was the pour of water into water that was simulating the water coming off the table. I used the same fish tank but moved it back by the table so it would have the same light on it as the real room shot. Then I put black fabric behind the fish tank to isolate the water. I set the self-timer on the camera and poured water into the tank as the shutter was fired. It took roughly 30 images to get the one that was just right. Later, I'll explain how the water was placed into the layered file.

The other components needed for the image were photos of a fish and a rug. For its own safety, the fish was shot separately from the shot with the girl. I'd first thought of shooting it with the model, but the water from the hose was so cold the poor things would die before the shoot was done.

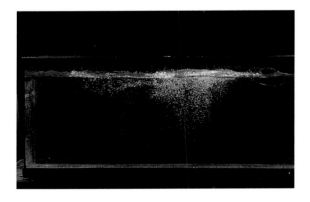

The rug was shot in the fish tank to get the fringe floating. I also needed it to be distorted and to pick up the color cast that shooting through the water would create. This was also shot against black.

Another shot I had to do was a fast pour of water off the table. (Water off table.eps) The original photo of the girl really did have water coming out of the hose but wasn't fast enough to be dramatic. So for this image, I placed the hose right on the table to get a rush of water coming off the edge.

The last shot I needed was the hose running off of the table through the fish. The reason for this was because objects look very different under water and I wanted to shoot as many elements really underwater that I could. Next is the fun part and that is putting it all together.

Assembly of the elements

The first step in putting these together was to lay the 2 main shots over each other and see if it all lined up.

1. Open both the hose and the fish tank images.

2. Drag the fish tank image from its Layers palette to the main image.

3. The table and chairs unfortunately didn't line up exactly right, so I had to use the Transform tool (CTRL/⌘+T) to "squeeze" the lower layer in a little. Lining up the backs of the chairs above the waterline was the key here.

It still didn't line up perfectly, but that was ok because water distorts anyway.

Next I had to remove the shadows underneath the cabinet and around the table legs and chairs. Underwater there would be no harsh shadows.

4. I zoomed in on the affected area and, using a low opacity Clone Stamp tool, brushed over the shadows with nearby lighter flooring.

5. I also added some very light more general shadow with the Burn tool at an exposure of 5%

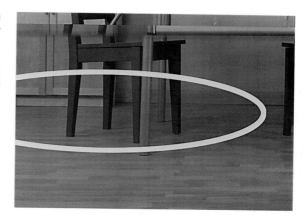

6. The next step was to clone the sides of the shot because the image did not go to the edges. This is a simple process, in this image of clean lines, of ensuring that the cloned area is exactly horizontal with the pasted area, and making a swift stroke up either side.

After that, I had to add the water lines from previous shots of the fish tank. This is an important detail and gave me the most trouble. I just wasn't sure how it would look in a real scenario... as if you were looking through a clear wall with a room half full of water. So it took a bit of playing.

Finally what seemed to work was the water line from the fish tank shot and then to diffuse it a bit. Basically I dropped that picture over the other layers, then used the Eraser to get the top edge right, and the Blur tool to get the bottom edge.

7. The extra hose shot was selected and copied over, then attached to a grouped adjustment layer to get the contrast and color right.

8. I used the Burn tool to darken down the lower half of the cabinet because it would be darker as the water got deeper.

9. Using a masked Hue/Saturation adjustment layer, I made the water bluer using the Colorize box but setting the layer to a low opacity.

Now the shot is taking a little shape. We have to add the pour of water into water, the water rushing off the table and the rug. The pouring water is taken from an additional series of two shots of flow, the hose repositioned each time.

10. The pour of water into water created lots of bubbles which would have been impossible to select individually. Instead, I placed the corner image, as shown.

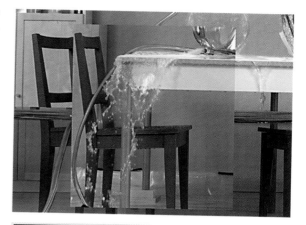

11. I then tucked it behind the tank shot in the Layers palette, and set a blending mode of Lighten that makes the black background invisible but retains the bubbles.

12. I used a second shot for the water off the table because one wasn't enough.

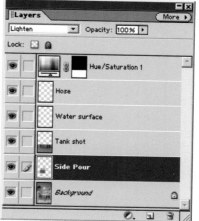

13. I also cut out the rug from another image and inserted it at this stage.

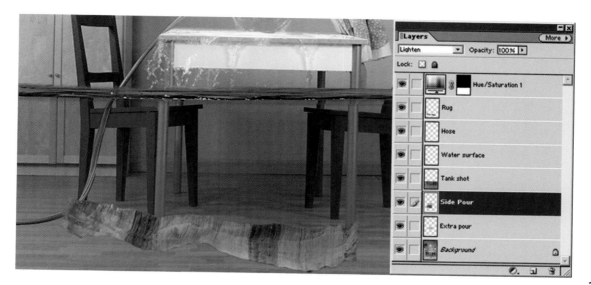

14. Using Lighten as the blending mode also works for the addition of the water into water shot.

Here you can see the layer in Normal blending mode and then in Lighten mode.

15. Shadows under the rug were added to a copy of the Tank Shot layer by using the Burn tool. Burning and Dodging is a trial and error method for which mode to use it in. The choices are highlights, midtones, or shadows. They have different effects depending on whether the subject is light or dark.

16. I also had to add a shadow underneath the hose because, if you remember, this hose image that runs through the water was added.

17. Next was to add some highlights to the floor which simulates a pattern that may be cast by the water. Using the Dodge tool, I randomly dodged parts of the floor being careful not to dodge any of the floor under the table.

Finally at this stage, I decided to increase the Opacity of my Hue/Saturation adjustment layer a little so the water looked more, and deeper blue.

Details

Details are very important. What really makes a shot work and believable are the details. Look closely at any image that looks real and that's what pulls the shot together. This is the point where the details to our flooded kitchen pull it together.

18. We need to make the girl's feet appear through the water. Using the Eraser tool to clear a space in the Tank Shot layer(s) and then the Clone Stamp tool to make any necessary repairs, we can make a perfect foot-sized gap so that they appear beneath the surface of the water.

Have you ever noticed that objects that are recently submerged emit tiny bubble as the trapped air escapes from the object. So the next step was to add bubbles to the hose, around the chair legs and especially from the rug.

19. I duplicated the bubbles layer a few times, retaining its blending mode but reducing its opacity and using the Eraser tool to remove bubbles in different patterns.

The fish in the fishbowl during the photo shot with the model wasn't in the right spot. So the fish was shot separately, selected, and copied over into the fish bowl. But it didn't have the right distortion to match the turbulent water coming into the fish bowl. So I used a filter to distort it. Filter > Distort > Ripple. Then I softened the edges using the Blur tool.

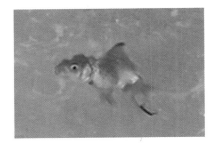

20. The fish near the floor had the same treatment. Outlined, the Ripple filter and again edges softened with the Blur tool.

And believe it or not that's it. That completes the shot!

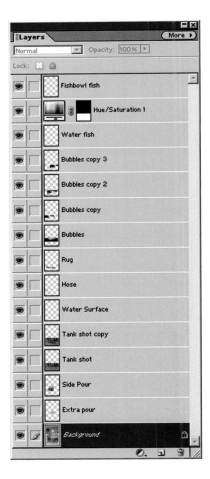

There is always a point at which I look at an image and ask myself, is it done? I'm never sure, but I have come to find that if you keep tweaking, it can be tweaked to death. If you do some imaging on your own, know when to stop. Usually when the photo doesn't gain anything from what you just did, it wasn't necessary. This kind of thing takes a lot of time, but if you love doing it, you won't mind how quickly the minutes seem to tick by, and you will end up with some awesome images.

I've been shooting photos for 20 years. But my real passion kicked in when I discovered the power of digital photography and Photoshop. In the last few years my business has gone 100% digital, right from capture. In the viewfinder are mostly kids and products. I probably spend too much time in Photoshop, but I have to admit that the program gives me an intoxicating level of control over the photos I shoot.

That control drew me in and made me take the program a little further, putting together finished images that used imaging in a subtle manner. I want the photos to be about the concept not about the Photoshop work, but the computer played a huge role in each image.

Most of my clients are presently catalog clients that have some Photoshop needs. The knowledge of the program has helped immensely in simple retouching. It's so surprising how fine the line is between the Photoshop details that make a shot look real versus having it look "Photoshoppy".

★ Hero

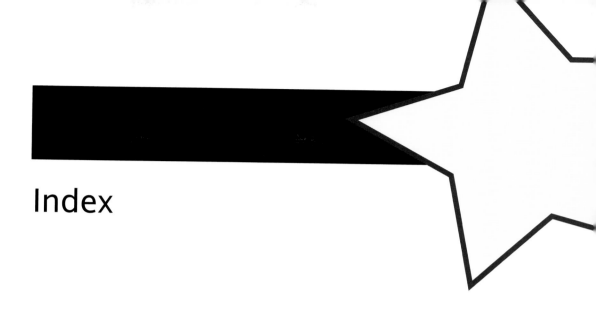

Index

The index is arranged hierarchically, in alphabetical order. Many second-level entries also occur as first-level entries. This is to ensure that you will find the information you require however you choose to search for it.

friends of ED particularly welcomes feedback on the layout and structure of this index. If you have any comments or criticisms, please contact: feedback@friendsofed.com

A

Add to selection button 49
additive color 5
Adjustment layers 74
  individual adjustments 79
  levels adjustments 75
  list 77, 78
  photograph manipulation 108
aging images 162-164
alpha channels 6
anti-aliasing 55, 56
Arah, Tom 210
  See also Paris by night
  (tutorial)
Auto Contrast command 188
Auto Levels command 36, 188

B

background layers 78
backlighting adjustment 41
batch processing 181
Beckham, Barry 238
  See also busker (tutorial);
  resolution (tutorial)
blending modes 82, 191
  brushes 151
  Color blending mode 89
  Color Burn blending mode 85
  Color Dodge blending
   mode 86
  Darken blending mode 84
  Difference blending mode 88
  Dissolve blending mode 84
  Exclusion blending mode 88
  Hard Light blending mode 87
  Hue blending mode 88
  Lighten blending mode 85
  Linear Burn blending mode 85
  Linear Dodge blending
   mode 86
  Linear Light blending mode 87
  Luminosity blending mode 89
  Multiply blending mode 84,
   163
  Normal blending mode 84
  Overlay blending mode 86

Saturation blending mode 88
  Screen blending mode 85
  Soft Light blending mode 86
  Vivid Light blending mode 87
Blur tool 102
Bob (tutorial) 92-95
Brightness/Contrast slider 31
Brush tool
  blending modes 151
  Color Jitter option 152
  Color Picker 148
  Fade option 152
  Hardness option 152
  Impressionist Brush tool 152
  More Options button 151
  opacity 151
  Options bar 150
  Scatter option 152
  sizes 151
  Spacing option 151
brushes 200
Burn tool 102, 262
  See also Dodge tool
busker (tutorial) 234-237
  Cutout filter 235
  duplicating layers 234
  Eraser tool 236
  flattening layers 237
  merging layers 236
  opacity 236
  Plastic Wrap filter 235

C

cameras 244
Clone Stamp tool 112
  difficult areas 100
  distracting objects 245, 246
  Options Bar 99
  spot removal 98
Clouds filter 230
color 30
  See also spot color (tutorial)
  additive color 5
  alpha channels 6
  brightness and contrast
  adjustments 31
  color casts 36-38

Color Picker 148, 149
  color spaces 5
  ICC color profiles 6
  printing 6
  recoloring images 42
  selections using Magic
  Wand tool 54
  spot color 164
  subtractive color 6
Color blending mode 89
Color Burn blending
mode 85
Color Dodge blending
 mode 86
Color Picker 148, 149
color spaces 5
Color Variations dialog 37
composition 239, 241, 242
compression 186
Craquelure filter 231, 232
Create Web Photo Gallery
Option 178-180
Crop tool 27
cropping images 27, 29, 30
Custom Shape tool 142, 204

D

Darken blending mode 84
Deselect option 48
Difference blending
mode 88
Dissolve blending mode 84
Dodge tool 263
  See also Burn tool
Dry Brush filter 214

E

effects
See also filters
  aging images 162
  blizzard layer 160
  Effects palette 15, 159
  flattening layers 161
  layer effects 161
  Vignette effect 161
Effects palette 15, 159
Ellipse tool 143

Elliptical Marquee tool 47
Eraser tool 236
Exclusion blending mode 88
Expand option 61
exporting images
  batch processing 181
  Create Web Photo Gallery
  option 178
  File name box 174
  JPEG options 174
  layers 81
  PNG options 174
  Save As option 173
  Save for Web option 175
  TIFF options 174

F

family photo (tutorial) 109-114
See also happy snaps (tutorial)
  adjustment layers 113
  background image 109
  Clone Stamp tool 112
  Dodge and Burn tools for
  shadows 114
  duplicating layers 112
  eye movement 113
  feathering selection 110
  Free Transform tool to scale
  image 111
  moving image behind
  others 111
  reducing flash 113
  selection 110
feathering 56
File Browser 11, 24
file formats 18, 81, 176
Fill Flash option 40
filters 189, 212
See also effects; resolution
(tutorial); watercolor
(tutorial)
  applying to layers 154
  Filters palette 154
  Gaussian Blur filter 156, 162
  Liquify filter 156, 157, 158
  plug-in filters 192
  previewing filters 155

settings 155
  Sharpen filters 156
  Stroke Pressure option 155
  Undo History palette 190
  Unsharp Mask filter 163
Filters palette 14
Flatten Image option 80
focus sharpening 44
formats 244
frames 227, 228
Free Rotate Layer option 26
Free Transform tool 60-62

G

Gaussian Blur filter 156, 162
girl and fish (tutorial) 253-265
  adding bubbles 263
  assembling pictures 257
  Burn tool for shadows 264
  Clone Stamp tool to
  remove shadows 259
  concept 255
  Dodge tool 263
  Eraser tool to show feet 263
  Hue/Saturation adjustment
  layer 260
  Lighten blending mode 260
  photography 255, 256
  pouring water 260
  Ripple filter to distort 264
  water line adjustments 259

H

happy snaps (tutorial) 239-251
  blurring background 243
  Clone Stamp tool 245
  composition 239, 241
  distracting objects 245
  Gaussian Blur filter 243
  Levels Adjustment layer
  243, 249
  lighting 247
  lining up photos 240
  motion 248
  Motion Blur filter 248
  simplifying photo 240

Hard Light blending
  mode 87
Hints palette 13
How To palette 13
Hue blending mode 88
Hue/Saturation adjustment
  layers 230

I

ICC (International Color
  Consortium) color profile 6
image adjustments 23
  brightness and contrast
  adjustments 31
  color casts 36
  cropping images 27
  lighting problems 39
  recoloring images 42
  rotating images 24
  sharpening images 44
image preparation 184
images 17
  adjustments 23
  aging 162
  exporting 173
  file formats 18
  formats 244
  opening 17
  preparation 184
  resizing 20, 186
  resolution 186
  saving 21
Impressionist Brush
  tool 152, 153
Info palette 15
interface 8
Inverse option 50

J

JPEG files 18, 174, 186

L

Lasso tool 50, 110
layer masks 76
layer styles
  Layer Styles palette 89
  removing styles 92

shapes 143
text and images 137, 138
Layer Styles palette 17, 89
Bevels option 91
Clear Styles icon 92
preset styles 90
Style Settings dialog 92
layers 65, 197
See also **Bob (tutorial)**
Adjustment layers 74, 79
background layers 78
blending layers 235
compositing 198
creating new layers 70
cropping images 27
duplicating layers 72
exporting images 81
flattening images 80
layer styles 89
Layers palette 67
linking layers 69, 73
masking layers 76
merging layers 73, 237
moving layers 70
naming layers 78
non-destructive editing 66
rotating images 25
saving layers 81
transparency 73
Layers palette 17, 67
Create a new layer button 70
Create New Adjustment
Layer button 74
customizing palette 69
diagram 68
Duplicate Layer option 72
Flatten Image option 80
Merge Down option 80
Merge Linked option 73
Merge Visible option 80
More menu 70
moving layers 71
Opacity slider 74
Type layer appearance 131
Levels panel
Auto Levels option 36
eyedroppers, using for

quick levels 34
highlights slider 33
lowlights slider 32
midtones slider 33
Output Levels slider 34
Lighten blending mode 85, 261
lighting 40-41, 247
Line tool 143
Linear Burn blending mode 85
**Linear Dodge blending
 mode 86**
**Linear Light blending
 mode 87**
Liquify filter 156, 157, 158
Luminosity blending mode 89

M

Magic Wand tool 53, 110
Magnetic Lasso tool 53, 54
Marquee tools 46, 47, 49
masks 76, 77
Merge Down option 80
Merge Visible option 80
merging photographs *See*
Photomerge
motion 248
Move tool 60, 72
**Multiply blending mode
 84, 163**

N

Navigator palette 15
Noise filter 231
Normal blending mode 84

O

opacity 151
Options Bar 28, 54
Overlay blending mode 86

P

palettes 11
Effects palette 15
Filters palette 14
Hints palette 13
How To palette 13
Info palette 15

Layer Styles palette 17
Layers palette 17, 67
Navigator palette 15
Palette well 10
Swatches palette 16
Undo History palette 16
panoramas *See* **Photomerge**
**Paris by night (tutorial)
183-209**
Auto Levels command 188
background color 193
blending modes 191
Brush tool 201
Brushed Metal pattern 197
Collage filter 193
color correction 208
compositing 197
Custom Shape tool 204
Dissolve blending mode
 203, 207
Drop Shadow effect 196
Dry Brush filter 190
editing text 195
finishing touches 207
fireworks 2 layer 202
fireworks 3 layer 202
Fireworks layer 201
Fresco filter 190
Hue/Saturation adjustment
layer 208
image preparation 184, 185
image size 187
layer creation 198
layer naming 206
layers and filters 191
opacity 207
plane layer 205
selection 198
shapes, adding to montage
 205
sky gradient 100
text 195
Vapour Trails layer 208
perspective 122
Perspective tool 63

photograph manipulation 97
See also **family photo (tutorial); sky (tutorial); younger (tutorial)**
   Blur tool 102
   Burn tool 102
   Clone Stamp tool for spot removal 98
   Dodge tool 101
   Photomerge 120
   Red Eye Brush tool 104
   Sharpen tool 103
   Smudge tool 103
   Sponge tool 103
   texture changes 102
Photomerge 120
   Advanced Blending option 123
   Clone Stamp tool 126
   cropping image 126
   Cylindrical Mapping option 123
   gradient to mask sky 125
   levels adjustment layer 124
   panorama creation 121
   perspective correction 122
   Set Vanishing Point tool 122
Photoshop Elements 2 1, 211
   interface 8
   Mac versus PC 3
Picture packages 172, 173
Pierson, Todd 265
   See also **girl and fish (tutorial)**
Pin Light blending mode 87
Plastic Wrap filter 235
PNG files 174
Polygon tool 143
Polygonal Lasso tool 51
printing 6
   Center Image box 169
   Contact Sheet option 170, 171
   image size 168
   index prints 170
   margins 168
   Output options 170
   Page Setup options 168
   Print Preview dialog 170

resolution 169
Show More Options button 170
PSD files 18

R

Rectangle tool 143
Rectangular Marquee tool 49
Red Eye Brush tool 104, 105
Replace Color option 42
Reselect option 48
resizing images 20
resolution 7
   resolution (tutorial) 213-215
Ripple filter 265
rotating images
   cropping and rotating simultaneously 29
   File Browser 24
   Free Rotate Layer option 26
   layers 25
   opened images 25
   quality of images after rotation 29
Rounded Rectangle tool 143

S

Saturation blending mode 88
Save for Web option
   Browser Dither 175
   Create Web Photo Gallery option 178
   file formats 176
   image size 175
   quality 177
saving images 21, 81
Screen blending mode 85
selection
   Add To Selection button 49
   angular shape selection 51
   anti-aliasing 55
   automatic shape selection 52
   complicated shape selection 48
   Contract Selection option 110
   copying selections 60
   deselecting areas 47

   feathering selections 56
   inverting selections 50
   Lasso tool 50
   Magic Wand tool 54
   Magnetic Lasso tool 53
   Marquee tools 46
   moving selections 59
   Polygonal Lasso tool 51
   Selection Brush tool 57
   switching tools 49
   transforming selections 60
Selection Brush tool 57
Set Vanishing Point tool 122
Shape Selection tool 142
shape tools 141
   See also **wrench (tutorial)**
   creating shapes 143
   Custom Shape tool 142
   Ellipse tool 143
   layer styles 143
   Line tool 143
   Options bar 142
   Polygon tool 143
   Rectangle tool 143
   Rounded Rectangle tool 143
   Shape Selection tool 142
Sharpen filters 156
Sharpen tool 103
Shipley, Paul 251
   See also **happy snaps (tutorial)**
shortcut keys 77
Shortcuts bar 9, 24
sky (tutorial) 106-109
   Background layer visibility 106
   Chapter04eg03sky.psd 107
   feathering selection 106
   flattening layers 109
   grouping layers 108
   levels adjustment layer 108
   new sky layer 107
Smart Blur filter 218
Smudge tool 103
Soft Light blending mode 86
Soft Light filter 219
Sponge tool 103

spot color (tutorial) 164-166
Straighten and Crop Image
 option 30
subtractive color 6
Swatches palette 16

T

text 127
See also **words from
pictures (tutorial)**
 adding text to documents
 129
 displaying text 128
 images and text 137
 layer styles 137, 138
 rasterizing text 132
 shaping text 132
 text editors 131
 Type tool 129
 word processor text 131
Texture filters 226
TIFF files 18, 174
Tool Options bar 10
Toolbox 9, 27
**transforming selections
 60-63**
Type tool
 editing text 194
 formatting text 195
 Horizontal Type tool 130
 Layers palette 131
 Options Bars 129
 Warp Text button 132

U

**Undo History palette
 16, 190**
URLs
 www.bbdigital.co.uk 211
 www.designer-info.com 183
 www.jasc.com 192
 www.sapphire-
 innovations.com 192

V

**Vivid Light blending mode
 87**

W

Warp Text button 133-136
**watercolor (tutorial)
 215-233**
 artistic filters 220
 Burn tool 225
 canvas resizing 229
 Clone tool 217
 Clouds filter 230
 color sampling 230
 Craquelure filter 231, 232
 cropping image 216
 duplicating layer 217
 feathering selection 221
 flattening layers 220, 224
 frames 227, 228
 Hue/Saturation adjustment
 layer 230
 Invert adjustment 219
 levels adjustment 217
 Noise filter 231
 patch technique 223, 224
 pavement selection 221
 renaming layer 218
 Smart Blur filter 218
 Soft Light filter 219
 Texture filters 226
 tone adjustments 220
web
 photo galleries 178
 saving images for web 175
**words from pictures
 (tutorial) 139-141**
wrench (tutorial) 143-146
 Add to shape area
 button 145
 Combine button 144
 copying shapes 144
 layer styles 145
 Polygon tool to create
 hexagon 144
 resizing image 146
 rotating shape 145
 Shape Selection tool 144
 Subtract from shape area
 button 144

Y

younger (tutorial) 114-119
 blemish removal 117
 Burn tool for darkening
 lips 117
 Clone Stamp tool 115, 116
 Dodge tool for lightening
 teeth 117
 duplicating background
 layer 115
 feathering selection 118
 Gaussian Blur filter 118
 levels adjustment 114
 lightening areas 117
 soft layer 118
 Sponge tool 117

Z

Zoom tool 18, 50